ICONS

IO.. B.... PIRANESI
VENET. ARCHITECTUS

F. Polanzani faciebat 1750 Super. permissu.

Luigi Ficacci
Istituto Nazionale per la Grafica, Roma

Giovanni Battista

PIRANESI

Selected Etchings
Eine Auswahl der Kupferstiche
Une sélection des eaux-fortes

TASCHEN

KÖLN LONDON MADRID NEW YORK PARIS TOKYO

Contents · Inhaltsverzeichnis · Sommaire

The Discovery of Rome

Die Entdeckung Roms aus dem Geiste Piranesi

out of the Spirit of Piranesi

La découverte de Rome dans l'esprit de Piranesi

LUIGI FICACCI

Giovanni Battista Piranesi was first and foremost an architect, although he disposed over a vast repertoire of exceptional skills in various technical fields and arts. A master draftsman of both imaginary and real subjects, as well as of architecture and stage design, Piranesi was also expert in the theory and practice of engineering and geometry. In addition, he was an extraordinary etcher. But he was convinced that it was only through architecture that he could exploit all his talents and revolutionize the world, that is, the manner and places in which people lived. To realize his ambition, he moved to Rome, the city that became the focus of his artistic work. For Piranesi, living amidst the remains of ancient Rome was the equivalent of dwelling at the center of civilization. He devoted himself to the rebuilding of modern Rome, which he felt had become degraded, corrupt, frivolous, and unworthy of its past. His goal was nothing less than the restor-

ation of the Eternal City to the magnificence of its ancient splendor –
a dream of unheard-of dimensions for its age. Alas, his artistic project
fell victim to the limitations of contemporary reality and remained incomplete upon his death. What we most appreciate in Piranesi today
– his genius as an engraver and inventor of a new conception of the
genre of the veduta, or architectural vignette – was for him nothing
more than a response to the exigencies of his situation. Piranesi's
work as engraver offered him not only a means of financial support,
but also a forum to present his ideas publicly, and thus garner the au-
thority that would permit him to carry on with his ultimate mission as
an artist: to restore the architecture of Rome, and thus its way of life
and society, to the standards of ancient times.

However, the total commitment of Piranesi's genius and technical
talents to the realization of his dream world required extraordinary re-

*war, der Ewigen Stadt wieder die Größe zu verleihen,
die sie in der Antike innehatte. Gemessen an der Rea-
lität seiner Zeit war dieses Vorhaben geradezu tita-
nisch. Und letztlich musste die konsequente Verwirklichung seines künstlerischen Projektes an dem starken
Widerstand der damaligen Gesellschaft scheitern. Obwohl Piranesi heute vor allem als genialer Stecher und
Erfinder einer neuen Konzeption des künstlerischen
Genres der „Vedute" geschätzt wird, war dieser Bereich
seiner künstlerischen Tätigkeit für ihn selbst nur eine
Notlösung. Denn seine Arbeit als Stecher sollte ihm
einerseits das Überleben sichern und andererseits die
Möglichkeit geben, seine Ideen darzulegen und sich
einen Namen zu machen, um im weiteren dem nachge-
hen und das mitteilen zu können, was ihm künstlerisch
am meisten am Herzen lag: Rom eine Architektur und
somit ein Leben und eine Gesellschaft zurückzugeben,
die der antiken Tradition dieser Stadt angemessen war.*

*Um seine vielseitige Begabung und seine techni-
schen Fertigkeiten der Gestaltung einer Welt widmen
zu können, die seiner eigenen Vorstellung entsprach,
bedurfte es außerordentlicher Mittel. Piranesi benötigte*

dégradée, corrompue, frivole, indigne de son passé.
Il rêvait de restituer à la Ville éternelle son lustre et
sa magnificence antiques – un projet titanesque s'il
en est, considérant la réalité de son époque. Réalité
dont la résistance finit du reste par prévaloir, empê-
chant Piranesi de réaliser la totalité de son projet artistique. Ce qu'aujourd'hui nous apprécions le plus
en cet artiste – son génie de graveur à l'eau-forte,
son aptitude à réinventer le genre artistique de la
« veduta » – tout cela ne fut pour lui que solutions
de secours. Son œuvre de graveur n'est qu'un
moyen de survie auquel il recourut non seulement
dans le souci de démontrer ses idées, mais aussi en
vue d'obtenir les ressources économiques et l'autori-
té artistique qui lui permissent d'approfondir et de
proclamer l'idée à laquelle il consacrait alors la
meilleure part de son énergie artistique : il fallait re-
donner à Rome une architecture, c'est-à-dire une vie
et une société qui soient à la hauteur de son passé
antique.

Toutefois, pour dédier l'intégralité de son génie
et de son talent technique à l'édification d'un

sources: he needed not only the full support of society, but also a patron of the stature and historical vision of a Caesar. Instead, he saw himself confronted with an inane society incapable of appreciating the grandeur of his imagination – and his fellow citizens returned the compliment by branding him an eccentric, a man out of touch with reality and all sense of measure. The enormous body of prints that Piranesi produced, illustrating and reconstructing ancient Rome, was nothing more than a rhetorical device to demonstrate the truth of his intellectual and artistic arguments concerning the past and a utopian transformation of the present. The theoretical and polemical tracts accompanying Piranesi's engravings, his entrepreneurial activities as a publisher, collector, restorer, and merchandiser of ancient relics – in other words, everything that historians focus on today for a fuller understanding of his greatness as engraver – were nothing more than

nicht nur die uneingeschränkte Unterstützung der Gesellschaft seiner Zeit, sondern auch einen mächtigen Auftraggeber, der wie die römischen Kaiser der Antike willens war, einen historischen Auftrag zu erfüllen. Aber er lebte in einer von ihm als bedeutungslos eingeschätzten Gesellschaft, die nicht in der Lage war, die Größe seiner Ideen zu erkennen. Man hielt ihn im Gegenteil für einen Traumtänzer, für einen, der jeglichen Realitätssinn und das Gespür für das richtige Maß verloren hatte. Sein umfangreiches Werk mit Ansichten und Rekonstruktionen antiker römischer Bauwerke diente ihm nur als Beweisführung für die Wahrheit seiner intellektuellen und künstlerischen Thesen, die sowohl die Kenntnis der Vergangenheit als auch die Utopie der Veränderung der Gegenwart betrafen. Seine polemischen theoretischen Abhandlungen und seine Tätigkeit als Verleger, Sammler, Restaurator und Händler antiker Fundstücke, das heißt all das, womit sich die kunstgeschichtliche Forschung zum besseren Verständnis seiner außerordentlichen Leistung als Kupferstecher gegenwärtig intensiver beschäftigt, betrachtete Piranesi in Wirklichkeit nur als Vorarbeiten und be-

monde à l'image de son idée créative, Piranesi avait besoin de moyens extraordinaires, par exemple de l'appui absolu de son époque, et surtout d'un commanditaire puissant, susceptible de porter sur ses seules épaules un engagement historique comparable à ce que fut le dessein des Césars dans la Rome antique. Or, il avait autour de lui une société qu'il jugeait inepte, incapable de reconnaître la grandeur de sa pensée ; et qui lui rendait son mépris, puisqu'elle l'avait catégorisé comme un exalté n'ayant ni le sens de la réalité ni celui de la mesure. Son importante production chalcographique, qu'il s'agisse d'illustrations ou de reconstitutions de la Rome antique, ne fut que la matière d'un plaidoyer infatigable visant à démontrer la vérité de ses arguments tant intellectuels qu'artistiques et touchant aussi bien à la connaissance du passé qu'à l'utopie d'un présent réformé. Les traités théorico-polémiques accompagnant ses gravures, ses activités d'ordre économique, en tant qu'éditeur, collectionneur, restaurateur et négociant de pièces archéologiques antiques – en bref, tout ce dont se nourrit

the props and backdrop for the great architectural works that he, the Palladio of his time, was unable to build. Nevertheless, both his reconstructions of the ancient city, which functioned as a theoretical manifesto, as well as his engravings executed primarily in response to market demand – such as his views of contemporary Rome – mark a radical break with tradition. His prints enabled people "see" in a new and theretofore unimaginable way. Whatever the subject of the scene, the vedutas revealed something unknown, whether they depicted original architectural creations, or caprices of the imagination, or decorative models of amazing complexity. Even his illustrations of the relics, techniques, or unfamiliar tools of the ancient world were always represented with a precision and decisiveness that rendered all previous reproductions obsolete. Similarly his engravings of famous landscapes or of monuments already familiar to European culture pre-

gleitende Maßnahmen für sein großes Lebenswerk als Architekt, als Palladio seiner Zeit, ohne allerdings dieses Ziel je verwirklichen zu können.

Dennoch stellten sowohl seine als theoretisches Manifest verstandenen Rekonstruktionen des antiken Rom als auch der an den Bedürfnissen des Marktes orientierte Teil seines Werkes, so zum Beispiel die Ansichten des modernen Rom, einen ausgesprochen radikalen Bruch mit der Tradition dar, da seine Stiche sich durch eine unbekannte und bis dahin überhaupt nicht vorstellbare Sichtweise auszeichneten. Unabhängig von ihrem Sujet offenbarten sie stets etwas Unbekanntes, ganz gleich, ob es sich um eigenständige Architekturentwürfe, imaginäre Bauwerke oder Dekorationsmuster von erstaunlicher Formenvielfalt handelte. Selbst seine Illustrationen von Fundstücken, Darstellungen von Arbeitstechniken oder unbekannten, im Altertum benutzten Geräten wiesen eine Genauigkeit und Entschiedenheit in der Wiedergabe auf, die alle vorangegangenen Reproduktionen dieser Art in den Schatten stellte. Auch die von Piranesi gestochenen Tafeln mit Abbildungen berühmter Landschaften oder bekannter Bauwerke, die

l'historiographie moderne pour approfondir notre compréhension de son génie de graveur, tout cela n'était que les supports et les corollaires de son grand œuvre d'architecte, celui d'un Palladio de son époque, celui-là même qu'il ne réussira pas à porter à son terme. Néanmoins, que sa production soit argumentative ou documentaire, s'attachant en ce cas à la Rome antique, ou qu'elle cherche essentiellement à répondre aux exigences du marché, comme c'est le cas des vues de la Rome moderne, elle opère une rupture radicale avec la tradition. Les estampes de Piranesi donnaient à « voir » d'une manière jusqu'alors inédite et inimaginable. Quel que fût leur sujet, elles en dévoilaient chaque fois une dimension encore inconnue. Il s'agissait pour certaines d'inventions architecturales originales, de caprices de l'imagination, de modèles décoratifs d'une variété de formes extraordinaire. D'autres étaient des illustrations détaillant des objets, des techniques, des instruments du monde antique, parfois totalement inconnus, mais qu'elles présentaient avec une telle exactitude et une telle fermeté de dé-

sented a totally new way of seeing the object, resurrecting an utterly unknown world in which the precision of Piranesi's rendition makes every element identifiable but at the same time imbues it with a suggestive power that confronts the viewer with a new – and potentially unsettling – perspective. Piranesi's views of contemporary Rome are similarly awe-inspiring, even when they depict the most predictable subjects and represent a reality that Piranesi in fact disdained more than admired. Indeed, his way of illustrating contemporary monuments and urban environments that he himself considered mediocre nonetheless revolutionized the European visual imagination. In part, this was due to the artist's exceptional powers of observation, but also to the bold chromatic contrasts of light and shadow that exerted a psychological impact on the viewer. Last but not least there is the drama that Piranesi's incomparable skies lend to the scenes – not to mention

Teil der europäischen Kultur waren, vermittelten ein im Verhältnis zum bisherigen Erkenntnisstand vollkommen unbekanntes Bild, das heißt, sie gaben eine ganz neue Welt wieder, in der jeder bekannte Inhalt trotz der exakten Wiedergabe extrem suggestiv dargestellt und dadurch verfremdet wurde. Sogar die Ansichten des zeitgenössischen Rom wirkten ungewöhnlich, obwohl es sich dabei um gängige Sujets handelte, die eine Wirklichkeit widerspiegelten, der Piranesi eher kritisch als bewundernd gegenüber stand und die ihn deshalb kaum inspiriert haben dürfte. Dennoch beeinflussten seine Darstellungen von Bauwerken und Stadtansichten des modernen Rom, die er selbst im Grunde als mittelmäßig betrachtete, die in Europa herrschende Sichtweise entscheidend.

Dazu trugen seine außerordentliche Beobachtungsgabe bei, sowie der kühn durchgeführte Chromatismus von Licht und Schatten und die dadurch ausgelöste psychologische Wirkung auf den Betrachter. Bahnbrechend wirkte nicht zuletzt auch der unbeschreibliche Himmel, der diesen Szenarien etwas Dramatisches verlieh, ganz zu schweigen von den furchter-

cision formelle qu'elles vouaient à l'oubli toute reproduction antérieure. Quand bien même elle abordait une vue déjà célèbre ou un monument familier, archétype du patrimoine européen, une table réalisée par Piranesi en tirait une image tout à fait originale, sans commune mesure avec les reproductions précédentes. Et c'est bel et bien un monde nouveau, inconnu, que l'artiste dépeignait là, un monde où chaque élément de connaissance se trouvait étonnamment exaspéré, jusque dans l'exactitude de son rendu, de par un pouvoir de suggestion tout à fait exceptionnel. Il n'est pas jusqu'aux vues de la Rome moderne qui ne prissent sous son ciseau un caractère saisissant. Elles constituaient pourtant ses sujets les plus prévisibles, les plus emblématiques d'une réalité où son élan inventif trouvait plus de motifs d'objection polémique que d'admiration. Aussi médiocres que lui paraissaient parfois les édifices et les aménagements urbains de son époque, les représentations qu'il en fit provoquèrent une véritable explosion dans l'imaginaire visuel européen. On peut voir à cela des causes multiples, ne serait-

the terrifying people that populate them. He thus transforms all objects in his illustrations into a poetic fantasy that excites the imagination and simultaneously infuses it with a real and present image that challenges the observer's individual and existential awareness. For this reason, Piranesi's ability to stir the viewer's fantasy – to convey through his etchings a certain emotional apprehension of the ancient world and the city that for Piranesi most embodied it, namely Rome – had a greater and more enduring influence than his various theoretical treatises, which were only of passing importance in eighteenth-century Europe. More or less consciously, the subsequent romantic conception of antiquity and of Rome itself as "Roman" derives from the visual filter originally created by Piranesi. His was an understanding of antiquity as a living theme reflecting on the problems confronting our current existence.

regenden Menschen, die seine Bilder bevölkerten. Alle diese Elemente verwandelten jeden dargestellten Gegenstand in ein poetisches, die Phantasie anregendes Gebilde, das sich dem Betrachter einprägte, ja, ihn geradezu in seinem individuellen und existentiellen Selbstverständnis herausforderte.

Aus diesem Grund sollte Piranesis Gabe, die Vorstellungskraft des Betrachters anzuregen sowie eine gewisse emotionale Wahrnehmungsweise der antiken Welt und derjenigen Stadt, die die Antike nach Piranesi am meisten verkörpert – nämlich Rom – zu fördern, von größerem Einfluss sein als seine theoretischen Abhandlungen, die im zeitgenössischen europäischen Kontext nur vorübergehend von Bedeutung waren. Selbst seine qualitativ hochwertigen Entwürfe für Bauwerke und Einrichtungsgegenstände erzielten nicht dieselbe Wirkung. Die Tatsache, dass das römische Altertum und Rom selbst als romantisch und „romanhaft" wahrgenommen und erlebt werden, geht mehr oder weniger bewusst auf den von Piranesi mit seinen Stichen geschaffenen Filter zurück. Die Antike wird nach dieser Auffassung als ein lebendiges, mit der eigenen Existenz in Zusammenhang stehendes Phänomen betrachtet.

ce que son don exceptionnel d'observation ; ses tempêtes chromatiques d'ombres et de lumières, qui transfigurent les sujets dépeints, semblant les assujettir à l'impact du sentiment ; les ciels prodigieux qui bouleversent ces scènes ; ou encore la terrifiante humanité qui les anime. Sous l'effet conjugué de ces facteurs, le moindre objet représenté se mue soudain en vision poétique, stimulant l'imagination du spectateur et frappant son esprit comme un problème vibrant d'actualité ; voire même, un problème inhérent à sa conscience individuelle et existentielle de spectateur. C'est pourquoi, bien plus que la pertinence transitoire des thèses de Piranesi dans le contexte de l'érudition européenne de son époque, bien plus même que la qualité de ses inventions originales – qu'elles soient architecturales ou décoratives – c'est son pouvoir de suggestion sur l'imaginaire qui contribuera à générer, dans les siècles qui suivront, un mode d'appréhension tout émotionnel du monde antique et de la cité qui, selon l'artiste, en était le plus représentative : Rome. De façon plus ou moins consciente, c'est du filtre

The present volume is based on the comprehensive Taschen edition of *Piranesi*. *The Complete Etchings* by Luigi Ficacci, published by Taschen in 2000, and offers a selection of the most important images representing Piranesi's principal thematic series. Each of the series is prefaced by a bibliographical summary that provides full information on the composition of the work and its publishing history. The individual plates, in contrast, have been carefully chosen to represent the various aspects of Piranesi's figurative world and the fundamental principles of his formal language to the reader as clearly and synthetically as possible.

The plates from the *Vedute di Roma*, the first series devoted to the contemporary city, reveal the artist's exceptional ability to lend his engraved vedutas the same quality and descriptive force that had previously been realized only in painting. Never before had engraved land-

In der vorliegenden Ausgabe, zu deren Verwirklichung das im Taschen Verlag veröffentlichte Gesamtwerk der Kupferstiche Piranesis (Luigi Ficacci, Piranesi. The Complete Etchings, Köln 2000) herangezogen wurde, wird eine Auswahl der die wichtigsten thematischen Zyklen repräsentierenden Werke vorgelegt. Den verschiedenen Serien sind bibliographische Angaben über die jeweiligen Entstehungsdaten des Werkes und dessen Editionsgeschichte vorangestellt. Die einzelnen Bilder hingegen wurden so ausgewählt, dass die Elemente der Bilderwelt Piranesis sowie die Grundzüge seiner Formensprache dem Leser so eindrucksvoll wie möglich vermittelt werden.

Auf den Tafeln mit den Vedute di Roma, *dem Zyklus also, der die Ansichten des zeitgenössischen Rom zum Thema hat, wird Piranesis außergewöhnliche Fähigkeit deutlich, dem Kupferstich dieselbe Qualität und denselben Beschreibungscharakter zu verleihen, wie ihn das künstlerische Genre der „Vedute" bislang nur mittels der Malerei erreicht hatte. Denn bis zu diesem Zeitpunkt hatte es in der Radierung so großformatige und reichhaltige Landschaftsdarstellungen*

visuel de Piranesi que descend la perception « romanesque » et romantique de l'Antiquité romaine et de sa ville clé – cette manière d'attribuer une actualité et une permanence dans nos existences à une période historique révolue.

Le présent ouvrage est tiré de notre publication générale des œuvres complètes de Piranesi graveur à l'eau-forte (Luigi Ficacci, *Piranesi. The Complete Etchings*, éditions Taschen, Cologne 2000) et présente une sélection de ses estampes les plus significatives dans chacune des principales séries thématiques. Les séries retenues sont précédées d'une note bibliographique détaillant la composition complète de l'œuvre concernée et les différents épisodes de ses vicissitudes éditoriales. Quant aux estampes isolées, elles ont été choisies parmi celles présentant de la façon la plus synthétique et frappante les éléments qui composent le monde figuratif de Piranesi et les traits fondamentaux de son expression artistique.

Les tables des *Vedute di Roma*, séries dont la Rome contemporaine de l'artiste est la protagoniste, démontrent son talent unique, qui hissa la gravure

scape views been executed in such a large format and with such a wealth of nuanced chromatic values.

From Piranesi's immense collection of views of Roman antiquity – this huge project that dominated Piranesi's entire life – selected compositions illustrating both imaginary scenes and real places allow the reader to appreciate the artist's efforts to save the memory of Roman architecture from oblivion and express both the eloquent testimony of the ruins themselves and Piranesi's awe before the technological perfection and seemingly boundless dimensions of classical architecture. In these plates, the composition of the landscapes of ruin corresponds to their archaeological appeal, while the manner of execution expresses the artist's theoretical intentions and illustrates their scientific practicability. Indeed, these engravings possess an unprecedented beauty and passion, achieved through the artist's pioneering

mit derart abwechslungsreichen farblichen Nuancierungen noch nie gegeben.

Aus der umfangreichen Sammlung der Antichità Romane, *diesen titanischen Vorhaben, das Piranesi sein ganzes Leben lang beschäftigen sollte, wurden diejenigen Tafeln mit imaginären Sujets oder Reproduktionen realer Örtlichkeiten ausgewählt, auf denen das Bestreben des Künstlers erkennbar ist, die römische Architektur der Vergessenheit zu entreißen. Er bringt die Ruinen selbst zum Sprechen, nicht ohne die eigene Bewunderung angesichts der technologischen Perfektion und der gigantischen Dimensionen der klassischen Architektur zum Ausdruck zu bringen. Auf diesen Stichen entspricht die Komposition der Ruinenlandschaft Piranesis archäologischem Interesse, während der gewählte Stil die Absicht deutlich macht, eine Theorie und ihre wissenschaftliche Durchführbarkeit unter Beweis zu stellen. Denn die Schönheit dieser Kupferstiche, aber auch die Heftigkeit, mit der die Platte im Säurebad geätzt wurde, waren bis zu diesem Zeitpunkt vollkommen unbekannt. Die Exaktheit der Wiedergabe, die außerordentliche Fähigkeit, durch die kühne Technik*

à des sommets de qualité et de capacité descriptive que le genre artistique de la « veduta » n'avait atteint jusque-là que dans la peinture. Jamais, jusqu'à Piranesi, la gravure n'avait produit de paysages d'aussi grand format, d'une richesse aussi inépuisable et d'une telle mobilité de tons chromatiques.

Dans le cadre de l'immense travail d'illustration complète de l'Antiquité romaine entrepris par l'artiste – le projet colossal qui domina sa vie entière – sont présentées ici les compositions les plus représentatives des efforts de l'artiste, aussi bien dans les caprices de ses inventions que dans la reproduction de lieux réels, pour parvenir à son but : exhumer les souvenirs de l'architecture romaine du tombeau de l'ignorance, exprimer l'évidence « parlante » des ruines et son émerveillement devant la perfection technologique et la démesure de l'architecture classique. Dans ces tables, la composition paysagiste coïncide avec l'intérêt archéologique, et le style d'exécution se fait l'expression parfaite d'une intention théorique et de démonstration scientifique. L'exactitude de la reproduction peut

use of an extremely strong acid bath. The precision of Piranesi's reproduction, his exceptional ability to make the difficult technique of etching yield a highly faithful representation of the various materials used in the monuments, and to show the effects of aging create a powerful effect. The etched line, free and richly modulated, ceases to be a line and becomes a formative component of coloration. This produces an unprecedented emotional impact on the observer, who is drawn into the plane of representation, just as the main motif reaches out beyond the boundaries of the plate by force of its grandeur and evocative strength. In Piranesi, the new empiricism of archaeological science incorporates the power of the imagination and forges the two into a single unity. Each of his scientifically exact depictions thus bears a great metaphoric value, inseparably intertwined with artistic inspiration.

der Radierung eine möglichst wirklichkeitsgetreue Wiedergabe der Qualität der die dargestellten Bauwerke auszeichnenden Materialien und ihres Alterungsprozesses zu erzielen, wird bei Piranesi zu einer beeindruckenden visionären Emphase gesteigert. Die Zeichenführung ist so vielfältig abgestuft und fließend, dass sie nicht mehr als linear bezeichnet werden kann, sondern zum farbbildenden Element gerät. Der Betrachter wird emotional angesprochen und in die Darstellungsebene mit einbezogen, wobei das eigentliche Sujet durch seine imposante Größe und evokative Kraft geradezu über den Plattenrand hinaus strebt. Der gerade aufgekommene Empirismus der archäologischen Wissenschaft greift bei Piranesi auf die Kraft der Phantasie zurück und verschmilzt mit ihr zu einer untrennbaren Einheit. Jede wissenschaftliche Demonstration nimmt einen immensen metaphorischen Wert an und wird eins mit der künstlerischen Eingebung.

être qualifiée de prodigieuse, non moins que la maîtrise de Piranesi, capable de tirer de la technique ardue de l'eau-forte un rendu étonnamment fidèle des diverses textures et patines des matériaux associés dans les monuments représentés – le tout se fondant dans une bouleversante emphase visionnaire. L'entaille est traitée avec une variété extraordinaire de modulation et une totale liberté de flux, au point de ne plus pouvoir se définir comme ligne, mais bien comme élément constitutif de la couleur. Quant à l'impact sur le spectateur, jamais avant Piranesi il ne fut de nature aussi émotionnelle. L'observateur se retrouve en effet totalement impliqué dans le plan de la représentation – le sujet principal débordant du reste largement de son support, tant il est imposant et évocateur. Pour nouveau qu'il soit à l'époque, l'empirisme de la science archéologique atteint chez Piranesi la puissance de l'imaginaire. Mieux : il fusionne avec l'imaginaire et en devient indissociable. Chaque démonstration scientifique endosse une valeur métaphorique immense. Science et inspiration ne font plus qu'un.

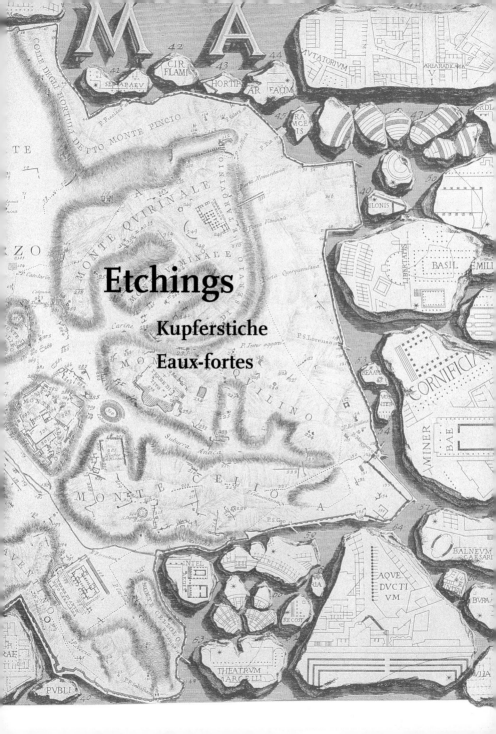

Etchings

Kupferstiche
Eaux-fortes

Prima Parte di Architetture, e Prospettive inventate, ed incise da Gio. Batt.a Piranesi Architetto Veneziano dedicate al Sig. Nicola Giobbe. In Roma, MDCCXLIII. Nella Stamperia de'Fratelli Pagliarini Mercanti Librari, e Stampatori

Edition Pagliarini Brothers, Rome 1743. The title engraved on the title page: *Part One of Architecture and Perspectives: Imagined and Etched by Gio. Batt.a Piranesi, Venetian Architect: dedicated to Nicola Giobbe*. At the end of the text section are the date and address of the edition in printed characters: "In Rome, MDCCXLIII. In the press of the brothers Pagliarini Mercanti Librari, e Stampatori". Composed of a title page and 12 plates without legend or numbering; 4 text pages. Extremely rare edition, known for the discrepancies amongst various copies due to incompleteness or differences in the sequence of plates. *Doric atrium* appears in only a few copies of this edition and is never used again in subsequent ones, perhaps because it was damaged or lost.

Edition in *Opere Varie*, Bouchard, Rome 1750: composed of a title page and 16 numbered plates complete with legends. In comparison with the previous edition (1743): 5 new plates; *Doric atrium* missing; numerous changes and revisions of previously published plates (in the title page, change in the title and elimination of the dedication: *Prima Parte di Architetture, e Prospettive inventate ed incise da Giambatista Piranesi architetto*

Ausgabe Gebrüder Pagliarini, Rom 1743. Titel in das Titelblatt gestochen: *Erster Teil der Architekturen und Ansichten gezeichnet und gestochen von Gio. Batt.a Piranesi, venezianischer Architekt, gewidmet dem Herrn Nicola Giobbe*. Am Ende des Textes Jahr und Verleger der Ausgabe in Drucklettern: „Rom MDCCXLIII. In der Druckerei der Gebrüder Pagliarini Mercanti Librari, e Stampatori". Zusammengestellt aus Titelblatt, 12 Tafeln ohne Legenden und ohne Numerierung sowie vier Textseiten. Die Ausgabe ist sehr selten, häufig unvollständig oder unterschiedlich in der Reihenfolge der Tafeln. Das *Dorische Atrium* erscheint in wenigen Exemplaren dieser Ausgabe und wird in den nachfolgenden nicht mehr aufgenommen, vielleicht war die Platte beschädigt oder verlorengegangen.

Ausgabe in *Opere Varie*, Bouchard, Rom 1750: Titelblatt und 16 numerierte, mit Legenden versehene Tafeln. Im Vergleich zu der Ausgabe von 1743 sind fünf neue Platten hinzugekommen, das *Dorische Atrium* fehlt; zahlreiche Veränderungen und Überarbeitungen bereits erschienener Platten. Im Titelblatt ist der Titel verändert und die

Edition des frères Pagliarini, Rome 1743. Titre gravé sur le frontispice : *Première partie d'architectures et de perspectives inventées et gravées par Gio. Batt.a Piranesi, architecte vénitien, dédiées à M. Nicola Giobbe*. Au bas du texte se trouvent la date et l'adresse de l'édition, en caractères typographiés : « Rome, MDCCXLIII. Imprimerie des frères Pagliarini Mercanti Librari, e Stampatori ». Ouvrage composé d'un frontispice, de douze planches sans légendes ni numérotation et de quatre pages de texte. Il s'agit d'une édition très rare, connue par des copies relativement différentes car incomplètes ou présentant les planches dans un ordre différent. La gravure l'*Atrium dorique* apparaît seulement dans quelques exemplaires de cette édition et ne figurera plus dans les éditions suivantes.

Edition dans *Opere Varie*, Bouchard, Rome 1750 : Ouvrage composé d'un frontispice et de 16 planches numérotées et pourvues de légendes. Par rapport à l'édition précédente (1743), on remarque l'addition de cinq nouvelles matrices ; l'*Atrium dorique* manque ; de nombreuses modifications et réélaborations des plaques déjà imprimées (dans le frontispice, changement du titre

veneziano, fra gli Arcadi Salcindio Tiseio; in the other plates, addition of separate engraved legends and Arabic numbering in the lower right).

Subsequent editions of the collection *Opere Varie* according to publishing history.

Widmung getilgt: *Prima Parte di Architetture, e Prospettive inventate ed incise da Giambatista Piranesi architetto veneziano, fra gli Arcadi Salcindio Tiseio;* in den übrigen Tafeln Hinzufügung der Legenden in separaten Druckplatten und der arabischen Numerierung am unteren rechten Rand.

Weitere Ausgaben entsprechen der Edition der *Opere Varie.*

et suppression de la dédicace : *Prima Parte di Architetture, e Prospettive inventate ed incise da Giambatista Piranesi architetto veneziano, fra gli Arcadi Salcindio Tiseio* ; dans les autres planches, ajout des légendes avec un cuivre séparé et de la numérotation en chiffres arabes, en bas à droite).

Diverses publications selon l'histoire éditoriale du recueil *Opere Varie.*

Prima parte di architetture, e prospettive …
355 x 250 mm

Title page: Part I of Architecture and Perspectives (1ˢᵗ state)

Titelblatt: Erster Teil der Architekturen und Perspektiven (1. Zustand)

Page de titre : Première partie d'architectures et perspectives (1ᵉʳ état)

PRIMA PARTE
DI ARCHITETTVRE
E PROSPETTIVE
INVENTATE ED INCISE
DA GIAMBATISTA PIRANESI
ARCHITETTO VENIZIANO
FRA GLI ARCADI
SALCINDIO TISEO

Ponte magnifico con Logge, ed Archi eretto da un Imperatore Romano, nel mezzo si vede la Statua Equestre del medesimo. Questo ponte viene veduto fuori di un arco d'un lato del Ponte che si unisce al sudetto, come si vede pure nel fondo un medesimo arco attaccato al principal Ponte.

Ponte magnifico...
240 x 360 mm

Magnificent bridge
Prachtvolle Brücke
Pont grandiose

Campidoglio antico a cui si ascendeva per cento gradini. Nel mezzo di questi gradini vi è una piazza sopra la quale vi stavano Ellefanti vestiti collo d'Toschi, ed altri orientali Vasi el Tempio fabbricato da Ottaviano Augusto nella guerra Cantabrica per voto fatto a Giove Tonante. Sopra il Frontispizio di questo Tempio vi era il medesimo Ottaviano in Cocchio tirato da quattro Cavalli. E sopra del medesimo vi stava lo Statue contanta del Senato per le imprese riportate Archi Trionfali Plaustri Longo, da pristina addotti in si comprano a Costana Archi trionfali colonne attornate da bassi rilievi, ed Cariationi degli Uomini Illustri, Tempi, Portici, ed il Pubblico Erario, come pure il Palazzo Capitolino Sopra lo pristina addotti vi stava traffei come Statua Equestre del Grande Augusto con Vasi, Statua, e trofei portati in trionfo.

Campidoglio antico...
240 x 360 mm

Ancient Capitol
Antikes Kapitol
Capitole antique

Tempio antico inventato e disegnato alla maniera di quelli che si fabbricavano in onore della Dea
Vesta; quindi vedesi in mezzo la grand'Ara, sopra della quale conservavasi dalle Vergini Vestali l'inestingui-
bile fuoco sacro. Tutta l'opera è Corintia ornata di statue e di bassi rilievi, e di altri ornamenti ancora
Il piano di questo Tempio è notabilmente elevato dal suolo: vedesi in mezzo la Cella rotonda, come lo è
pure tutto il gran Vaso del Tempio stesso: quattro loggie portavano ad essa, e per altrettante scale vi si
ascendeva. Le pareti del gran Tempio hanno due ordini, sopra il secondo s'incurva una vasta Cupola con
sfondati e rosoni e termina in una grande apertura, dalla qle dipende il lume alla Cella che le sta sotto.
Gio Batta Piranesi Archit.o ino, ed incise in Roma l'Anno 1773.   13.

Tempio antico...
345 x 250 mm

Ancient temple
Antiker Tempel
Temple antique

Mausoleo antico erello per le ceneri d'un Imperadore Romano. All'intorno di questo vi sono di Sepolcri piramidali
per altri Imperadori. Vi sono pure dell'Urne di Famigliari, delle anche Olle Sepolcrali in cui si pongono le loro
ceneri. Vi ne sono pure dell'altre pe' Servi, e Liberti. Questo Mausoleo è attorniato di magnifiche Scale, ai cui
piedi si vedono ornamenti Sepolcrali secondo il costume degli antichi Romani.   3.

Mausoleo antico ...
350 x 250 mm

Ancient mausoleum
Antikes Mausoleum
Mausolée antique

Ara antica sopra la quale si face.
Gio Batta Piranesi Architetto inventò, ed incise in Roma

anticamente i sagrifizi, con altre ruine all'intorno.

[Carceri]
Invenzioni Capric. di Carceri all'acquaforte datte in luce da Giovani Buzard in Roma Mercante al Corso

Edition Bouchard, Rome, s. a. (c. 1749/50): composed of a title page and 13 plates, of which 2 states are known:
First state: title on title page, *Fanciful Images of Prisons, etchings published by Giovani Buzard in Rome, conducting business on the Corso.*
Second state: title on title page, "Buzard", corrected as "Bouchard".
This edition is included in the collection *Opere Varie* (1750) and in some copies of *Le Magnificenze di Roma le più remarcabili* (s. a., c. 1751–1754).

Edition Piranesi, Rome, s. a. (c. 1761): composed of a title page and 15 plates, with the title: *Carceri d'invenzione di G. Battista Piranesi archit. vene.* (Imaginary Prisons of G. Battista Piranesi, Venetian Architect.)
Augmented by two new plates and a radical reworking of the engraving; addition of Roman numbering in the upper left.

Editions Paris: addition of numbers 349 to 364.

Ausgabe Bouchard, Rom, o. J. (um 1749/1750): Titelblatt und 13 Tafeln; zwei Zustände sind bekannt:
Erster Zustand: Titel im Titelblatt *Phantastische Entwürfe von Kerkern, in Kupfer gestochen und publiziert von Giovani Buzard, Buchhändler in Rom in der Via del Corso.*
Zweiter Zustand: im Titelblatt „Buzard" in „Bouchard" korrigiert.
Diese Ausgabe ist in den *Opere Varie* von 1750 enthalten und in einigen Ausgaben von *Le Magnificenze di Roma le più remarcabili* (o. J., um 1751–1754).

Ausgabe Piranesi, Rom, o. J. (um 1761): Titelblatt und 15 Tafeln unter dem Titel: *Carceri d'invenzione di G. Battista Piranesi archit. vene.* (Phantastische Entwürfe von Kerkern von G. Battista Piranesi, venezianischer Architekt.)
Die Ausgabe ist um zwei neue Tafeln erweitert, die Druckplatten wurden intensiv überarbeitet; Hinzufügung der römischen Numerierung oben links.

Ausgaben Paris: Hinzufügung der Nummern 349 bis 364.

Edition de Rome, Bouchard, s. d. (vers 1749/1750) : Ouvrage composé d'un frontispice et de 13 planches dont on connaît deux états :
1er état, titre sur le frontispice : *Images fantastiques de prisons gravées à l'eau-forte et publiées par Giovani Buzard à Rome, libraire sur le Corso.*
2e état, dans le titre sur le frontispice, « Buzard » a été corrigé en « Bouchard ».
Cette édition fait partie du recueil *Opere Varie* (1750) et de certains exemplaires de *Le Magnificenze di Roma le più remarcabili,* s. d. (vers 1751–1754).

Edition de Piranesi, Rome, s. d. (vers 1761) : Ouvrage composé d'un frontispice et de 15 planches, avec le titre : *Carceri d'invenzione di G. Battista Piranesi archit. vene.* (Prisons imaginaires de G. Battista Piranesi, architecte vénitien.)
Elle a été augmentée de deux nouvelles planches et le gravé a été revu radicalement ; addition d'une numérotation en chiffres romains en haut à gauche.

Editions de Paris : addition des numéros 349 à 364.

Invenzioni Capric[ciose] di Carceri
545 x 410 mm

Title page: Fanciful Images of Prisons (1st state)
Titelblatt: Fantastische Entwürfe von Kerkern (1. Zustand)
Page de titre : Images fantastiques de prisons (1er état)

Carceri d'Invenzione di G. Battista Piranesi
545 x 410 mm

Title page: Imaginary Prisons of G. Battista Piranesi (2ⁿᵈ state)
Titelblatt: Erfundene Kerker von G. Battista Piranesi (2. Zustand)
Page de titre : Prisons imaginaires de G. Battista Piranesi (2ᵉ état)

[Carcere II]
555 x 420 mm

"The Man in the Rack"
„Mann auf der Folter"
«L'Homme sur le chevalet»

[Carcere III]
540 x 410 mm

"The Round Tower" (2nd state)
„Der runde Turm" (2. Zustand)
«La Tour circulaire» (2e état)

[Carcere IV]
550 x 410 mm

"The Grand Piazza" (2nd state)
„Der große Platz" (2. Zustand)
«La Grande Place» (2e état)

[Carcere V]
560 x 410 mm

"The Lion Bas-Reliefs"
„Basreliefs mit Löwen"
«Les Bas-reliefs aux lions»

[Carcere VI]
540 x 400 mm

"The Smoking Fire" (2nd state)
„Rauchendes Feuer" (2. Zustand)
«L'Incendie» (2e état)

[Carcere VII]
550 x 410 mm

"The Drawbridge" (2nd state)
„Die Zugbrücke" (2. Zustand)
«Le Pont-levis» (2e état)

[Carcere VIII]
545 x 400 mm

"The Staircase with Trophies" (2nd state)
„Treppe mit Trophäen" (2. Zustand)
«L'Escalier aux trophées» (2e état)

[Carcere IX]
550 x 405 mm

"The Giant Wheel" (2ⁿᵈ state)
„Das große Rad" (2. Zustand)
«La Roue géante» (2ᵉ état)

[Carcere X]
410 x 550 mm

"Prisoners on a Projecting Platform" (2ⁿᵈ state)
„Gefangene auf einer vorspringenden Plattform" (2. Zustand)
«Prisonniers sur un éperon» (2ᵉ état)

[Carcere XI]
405 × 545 mm

"The Arch with a Shell Ornament" (2nd state)
„Der Bogen mit dem Muschelornament" (2. Zustand)
«L'Arc décoré d'une coquille» (2e état)

[Carcere XII]
410 x 560 mm

"The Sawhorse" (2nd state)
„Das Sägepferd" (2. Zustand)
« Le Chevalet de torture » (2ᵉ état)

[Carcere XIII]
400 x 545 mm

"The Well" (2nd state)
„Der Ziehbrunnen" (2. Zustand)
«Le Puits» (2e état)

[Carcere XIV]
410 x 535 mm

"The Gothic Arch" (2nd state)
„Gotischer Bogen" (2. Zustand)
«L'Arc gothique» (2e état)

[Carcere XV]
405 x 550 mm

"The Pier with a Lamp" (2nd state)
„Pfeiler mit Lampe" (2. Zustand)
«Le Môle au lampadaire» (2e état)

[Carcere XVI]
405 x 550 mm

"The Pier with Chains"
(2nd state)

„Pfeiler mit Ketten"
(2. Zustand)

«Le Môle aux chaînes»
(2e état)

Le Antichità Romane opera di Giambattista Piranesi architetto veneziano divisa in quattro tomi ... Tomo primo ... In Roma MDCCLVI nella stamperia di Angelo Rotilj nel palazzo de'Massimi ... S. vendono in Roma dai Signori Bouchard e Gravier mercanti libraj al Corso presso San Marcello

First edition Bouchard and Gravier, Rome 1756, 4 volumes: *The Antiquities of Rome by Giambattista Piranesi, Venetian architect, divided in four volumes ... Volume one ... printed at Rome in 1756 at the printworks of Angelo Rotilj in Palazzo de'Massimi ... Sold in Rome by Messrs Bouchard and Gravier, Merchant Booksellers on the Corso at San Marcello.*

VOLUME I: Portrait of Piranesi engraved by Polanzani, 1 title page, 6 ornamented letters, 2 vignettes, 43 plates.
In an initial issue, the title page bears a dedication to Lord Charlemont; in a second, the dedication is deleted and replaced with *Urbis Aeternae Vestigia e Ruderibus Temporumque Iniuriis Vindicata Aeneis Tabulis Incisa I. B. Piranesius Venet. Romae Degens Aevo Suo Posteris et Utilitati Publicae*; the Charlemont coat of arms is also deleted. Some copies contain the portrait of Clement XIII engraved by Domenico Cunego (1757). In a third printing, the dedication varies and letters one and two to Lord Charlemont are inserted (1757).
Second edition, posthumous, Rome, 1784: same editor, with reference to Piranesi's title as knight, and the new address "in Roma MDCCLXXXIV nella stamperia Salomoni alla piazza di S. Ignazio".

Erste Ausgabe Bouchard und Gravier, Rom 1756, in vier Bänden: *Die Römischen Altertümer, Werk des Giambattista Piranesi, venezianischer Architekt, aufgeteilt in vier Bände ... Erster Band ... In Rom 1756 in der Druckerei von Angelo Rotilj im Palazzo de'Massimi ... Verkauft in Rom von den Buchhändlern Bouchard und Gravier an der Via del Corso in der Nähe von San Marcello.*

BAND I: Piranesis Porträt, gestochen von Polanzani, ein Frontispiz, 6 Initialen, 2 Vignetten, 43 Tafeln.
Der erste Zustand des Frontispiz enthält eine Widmung an Lord Charlemont; diese Widmung ist im zweiten getilgt und ersetzt durch *Urbis Aeternae Vestigia e Ruderibus Temporumque Iniuriis Vindicata Aeneis Tabulis Incisa I. B. Piranesius Venet. Romae Degens Aevo Suo Posteris et Utilitati Publicae*; getilgt ist auch das Wappen Charlemonts; in einigen Exemplaren findet sich das Porträt von Papst Klemens XIII., 1757 von Domenico Cunego gestochen; im dritten Zustand variiert die Widmung und der erste und zweite Brief an Lord Charlemont (1757) wurden aufgenommen.
Zweite, posthume Ausgabe, Rom 1784: Gleiche Fassung, mit

Première édition de Bouchard et Gravier, Rome 1756, quatre tomes : *Antiquités romaines, œuvre de Giambattista Piranesi, architecte vénitien ; divisée en quatre tomes ... Tome I ... A Rome 1756. Se vend à Rome à l'imprimerie Angelo Rotilj au palazzo de'Massimi ... Se vend à Rome chez les Signori Bouchard et Gravier libraires sur le Corso près de San Marcello.*

TOME I : Portrait de Piranesi gravé par Polanzani, 1 frontispice, 6 lettres ornées, 2 vignettes, 43 planches.
Dans un premier tirage, le frontispice porte une dédicace à Lord Charlemont ; dans un deuxième, la dédicace a été remplacée par : *Urbis Aeternae Vestigia e Ruderibus Temporumque Iniuriis Vindicata Aeneis Tabulis Incisa I. B. Piranesius Venet. Romae Degens Aevo Suo Posteris et Utilitati Publicae* ; l'emblème de Charlemont a également été effacé ; quelques exemplaires contiennent le portrait de Clément XIII, gravé par Domenico Cunego (1757) ; dans un troisième tirage, la dédicace est différente ; les lettres une et deux à Lord Charlemont (1757) ont été insérées. Deuxième édition posthume de Rome en 1784 : Même rédaction, avec la mention du titre de chevalier et la nouvelle adresse : « in Roma MDCCLXXXIV nella

In Vol. I, Piranesi's portrait by Polanzani has been replaced by a portrait drawn by Giuseppe Cades and engraved by Francesco Piranesi; the title page bears a dedication to Gustavus III, King of Sweden; composed of 43 plates plus title page; in some versions 3 plates by Francesco Piranesi follow, 2 of which are dated 1787.
Editions Paris: plates numbered from 1 to 229. The copperplates are preserved at the Calcografia dell'Istituto Nazionale per la Grafica, Roma (vols. I–IV).

VOLUME II: First and second edition, title on title page: *Le Antichità Romane di Giambatista Piranesi architetto veneziano tomo secondo contenente gli avanzi de' monumenti sepolcrali di Roma e dell'agro romano*. The volume consists of 63 plates, including the 2 title pages. Illustration numbers 226, 227, 228, 229, 234, 247, 249, 259, 260, with different abbreviations, bear the certification of authorship: "Barbault scolpì le figure".

VOLUME III: Title on title page: *Le Antichità Romane di Giamb. Piranesi archit. Venez. tomo terzo contenente gli avanzi de' monumenti sepolcrali di Roma e dell'agro romano*. Composed of 51 plates, including 2 title pages; 4 plates (not reproduced here) that, albeit unnumbered, occupy the spaces of numbers XXIII, XXIV, XXV, XXVI, engraved by Girolamo Rossi after a drawing by Antonio Buonamici; plates XXVII, XLVI, XLVIII bear, in different editions, the certification of authorship: "Barbault scolpì le

dem Hinweis auf den inzwischen erhaltenen Ehrentitel „cavaliere" sowie der neuen Adresse: „in Roma MDCCLXXXIV nella stamperia Salomoni alla piazza di S. Ignazio".
In Band I ist Polanzanis Piranesi-Porträt durch ein von Giuseppe Cades gezeichnetes und von Francesco Piranesi gestochenes Bildnis ersetzt worden; im Frontispiz eine Widmung an den König von Schweden, Gustav III.; insgesamt 43 Tafeln und ein Titelblatt; in einigen Exemplaren folgen 3 Tafeln von Francesco Piranesi, 2 sind 1787 datiert.
Ausgaben Paris: Die Tafeln sind von 1 bis 229 numeriert. Die Platten werden in der Calcografia in Rom aufbewahrt (Bände I–IV).

BAND II: Erste und zweite Ausgabe: *Le Antichità Romane di Giambatista Piranesi architetto veneziano tomo secondo contenente gli avanzi de' monumenti sepolcrali di Roma e dell'agro romano*. Zusammengestellt aus 63 Tafeln einschließlich der beiden Titelblätter. Die Abbildungsnummern 226, 227, 228, 229, 234, 247, 249, 259, 260 geben abgekürzt die Autorschaft an: „Barbault scolpì le figure".

BAND III: Titel im Titelblatt: *Le Antichità Romane di Giamb. Piranesi archit. Venez. tomo terzo contenente gli avanzi de' monumenti sepolcrali di Roma e dell'agro romano*. Zusammengestellt aus 51 Tafeln einschließlich der beiden Titelblätter; 4 Tafeln (hier nicht wiedergegeben) sind von Girolamo Rossi nach Zeichnungen von Antonio

stamperia Salomoni alla piazza di S. Ignazio».
Dans le tome 1 : un portrait dessiné par Giuseppe Cades et gravé par Francesco Piranesi a été substitué au portrait de Piranesi de Polanzani ; le frontispice porte une dédicace au roi de Suède, Gustave III ; 43 planches plus le frontispice ; dans certains exemplaires, se trouvent trois planches supplémentaires de Francesco Piranesi, dont deux datées de 1787.
Editions de Paris : Planches numérotées de 1 à 229. Les cuivres sont conservés à la Chalcographie de Rome (tomes I–IV).

TOME II : Première et deuxième édition : *Le Antichità Romane di Giambatista Piranesi architetto veneziano tomo secondo contenente gli avanzi de' monumenti sepolcrali di Roma e dell'agro romano*. 63 planches, y compris les deux frontispices. Les numéros des illustrations 226, 227, 228, 229, 234, 247, 249, 259, 260 avec des abréviations différentes portent la mention : « Barbault scolpì le figure ».

TOME III : Titre sur le frontispice : *Le Antichità Romane di Giamb. Piranesi archit. Venez. tomo terzo contenente gli avanzi de' monumenti sepolcrali di Roma e dell'agro romano*. 51 planches, y compris les deux frontispices ; quatre planches (non reproduites ici) ne portant pas de numérotation en chiffres romains, ont les numéros XXIII, XXIV, XXV, XXVI et ont été gravées par Girolamo Rossi d'après un dessin de Antonio Buonamici ; les planches XXVII, XLVI, XLVIII portent, dans des édi-

figure". The 1784 edition contains 54 plates.

VOLUME IV: Title on title page: *Le Antichità Romane di Giambattista Piranesi architetto Veneziano. Tomo quarto, contenente i ponti antichi, gli avanzi de' teatri, de' portici, e di altri monumenti di Roma* (ill. p. 79), Composed of 57 plates, including the 2 title pages. The 1784 edition contains 60 plates.

Buonamici gestochen. Obwohl diese Platten nicht numeriert sind, wurden die Nummern XXIII, XXIV, XXV und XXVI für sie vorgesehen; in den verschiedenen Ausgaben bezeichnen die Tafeln XXVII, XLVI und XLVII Barbault als Autor der gestochenen Figuren. Die Ausgabe von 1784 umfaßt 54 Tafeln.

BAND IV: Titel im Titelblatt: *Le Antichità Romane di Giambattista Piranesi architetto Veneziano. Tomo quarto, contenente i ponti antichi, gli avanzi de' teatri, de' portici, e di altri monumenti di Roma* (Abb. S. 79). Zusammengestellt aus 57 Tafeln einschließlich der beiden Titelblätter. Die Ausgabe von 1784 umfaßt 60 Tafeln.

tions différentes, la mention : « Barbault scolpì le figure ». L'édition de 1784 comporte 54 planches.

TOME IV : Titre sur le frontispice : *Le Antichità Romane di Giambattista Piranesi architetto Veneziano. Tomo quarto, contenente i ponti antichi, gli avanzi de' teatri, de' portici, e di altri monumenti di Roma* (ill. p. 79). 57 planches, y compris les deux frontispices. L'édition de 1784 comporte 60 planches.

Nobilissimo viro [...] Iacobo Caulfield de Charlemont... 460 x 680 mm

Title page to Vol. I with a dedication to Lord Charlemont (1st state)

Titelblatt Bd. I mit Widmung an Lord Charlemont (1. Zustand)

Page de titre du vol. I avec dédicace à Lord Charlemont (1er état)

Veduta del Pantheon
125 x 265 mm

View of the Pantheon
Ansicht des Pantheons
Vue du Panthéon

Veduta dell' interno del Pantheon

Piranesi Archit.dis.inc.

Veduta dell'interno del Pantheon
120 x 260 mm

Interior view of the Pantheon
Innenansicht des Pantheons
Vue intérieure du Panthéon

Avanzo del Tempio di Minerva Medica...
130 x 192 mm

Remains of the temple of Minerva Medica
Überreste des Tempels der Minerva Medica
Vestiges du temple de Minerva Medica

54

Veduta del Monumento del Condotto delle acque Claudia e Anione Nuovo. A. Speco dell'Anione Nuovo. B. Speco della Claudia. C. Condotto dell'Acqua Felice. D. Veduta interna della Porta Maggiore, la quale resta sotto uno de' due archi principali del monumento.

Piranesi Archit. dis. inc.

Veduta del Monumento del Condotto delle Acque Claudia e Anione Nuovo,
120 x 200 mm

The aqueduct of the Acqua Claudia and the Anio Nuovo
Das Aquädukt der Acqua Claudia und des Anio Nuovo
L'aqueduc de l'Acqua Claudia et de l'Anio Nuovo

STANZA sepolcrale scoperta, e demolita ci... ...an... e l'anno 1746 nella Vigna Casali a Porta S. Sebastiano. Le nicchie grandi delle facciate erano dipinte a grotteschi finte pietre di Stucchi.

Stanza sepolcrale...
118 x 192 mm

Tomb chamber
Grabkammer
Chambre funéraire

Una delle due Fornici di Stertinio nel Foro Boario
125 x 192 mm

One of the arches of Janus Quadrifons in the Forum Boarium
Einer der Bögen des Janus Quadrifons auf dem Forum Boarium
L'un des deux arcs de Janus Quadrifons au Forum Boarium

Avanzo degli archi
Neroniani sul monte
Celio...
115 x 256 mm

Remains of the
Neronian arches on
the Caelian Hill

Überreste der
Neronischen Bögen
auf dem Monte Celio

Vestiges des arcs de
Néron sur le mont
Caelius

A *Avanzo degli archi Neroniani sul monte*
nell' avanzo de' muri del castello dell

o ov' era la loro terminazione. B e C *Fistole e Cloache*
ua.

Piranesi Architetto diseg. incise

Veduta del second' ordine di una parte della Calcidica del Foro di Trajano. A Porta antica appartenente al terz'ordine. B Muro moderno. C Giardino del S.r Marchese Ceva. D Fabbriche moderne sopra le rovine del Foro di Nerva.

Piranesi Architetto dis. inc.

Veduta [...] di una parte della Calcidica del Foro di Trajano ...,
128 x 205 mm

View of a part of the exedra of Trajan's forum
Teilansicht der Exedra des Trajansforums
Vue d'une partie de l'exèdre du forum de Trajan

Fig. II.

B

C

Colonna Trajana. A Ripari fatti dal Pontefice Sisto V. al moderno piano di Roma. B Chiesa di S. Maria di Loreto. C Chiesa del Nome di Maria.

Piranesi Architett. dis. inc.

Colonna Trajana...
125 x 199 mm

Trajan's column
Trajanssäule
La colonne de Trajan

Avanzo del Tempio della Concordia
138 x 205 mm

Remains of the temple of Concord
Überreste des Concordia-Tempels
Vestiges du temple de la Concorde

A e B *Veduta degli Avanzi delle Case de Cesari sul Palatino.* C *Avanzi della Casa Augustana.* D *Avanzi della Casa Tiberiana.* E *Avanzi della Casa Neroniana.* F *Luogo ov' era il Circo Maſsimo.* G *Avanzi delle oſtruzioni de Sedili del medesimo Circo.* H *Marana e sia Acqua Crabra.*

Piranesi Architt: dis: inc:

Veduta degli Avanzi delle Case de Cesari sul Palatino...
136 x 274 mm

Remains of the palace of the Caesars on the Palatine
Überreste der Kaiserpaläste auf dem Palatin
Vestiges du palais des Césars sur le Palatin

Fig. II

Veduta dell' Arco di Costantino Magno. A. Avanzo della Meta Sudante. B. Vacuo del tubo della medesima. C. Avanzo del Palazzo de' Cesari sul Palatino. D. Chiesa di S. Bonaventura.

Piranesi Archit. dis. inc.

Veduta dell'Arco di Costantino Magno…

120 x 195 mm

View of the arch of Constantine
Ansicht des Konstantinsbogens
Vue de l'arc de Constantin

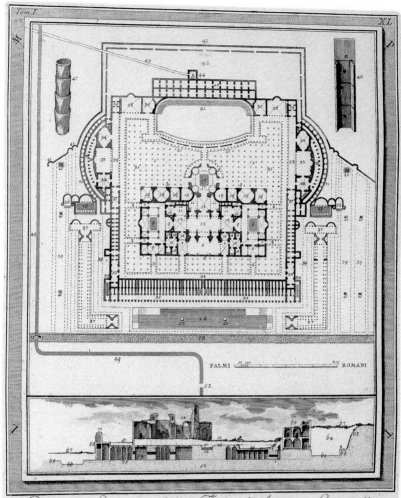

Pianta e Spaccato delle Terme d'Antonino Caracalla
275 x 235 mm

Plan and section of the baths of Caracalla
Grundriß und Schnitt der Caracalla-Thermen
Plan et coupe des thermes de Caracalla

**Antiquus bivii viarum
appiae at ardeatinae ...**
395 x 640 mm

Frontispiece: Ancient
intersection of the
Via Appia and Via
Ardeatina

Frontispiz: Kreuzung
der Via Appia Antica
und Via Ardeatina

Frontispice : Ancien
croisement de la via
Appia et de la via
Ardeatina

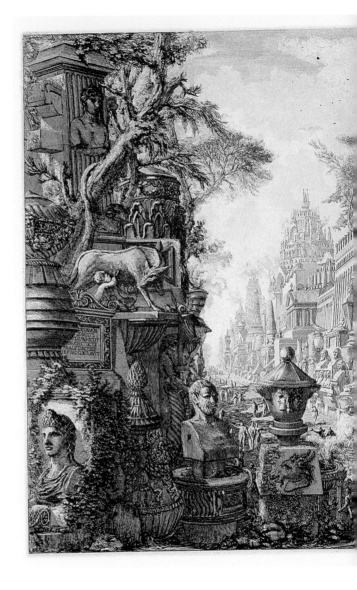

LIBERT ET
FAMILIAE
L. ARRVNTI·L·F
TER

Veduta dell'Ingresso della Camera Sepolcrale di L. Arrunzio...
395 x 600 mm

View of the entrance to the tomb chamber of L. Arruntius
Ansicht des Eingangs zur Grabkammer des L. Arruntius
Vue de l'entrée de la chambre funéraire de L. Arruntius

Veduta di altra parte della Camera Sepolcrale di L. Arrunzio ...
395 x 600 mm

View of another part of the tomb chamber of L. Arruntius
Ansicht eines anderen Bereichs der Grabkammer des L. Arruntius
Vue d'une autre partie de la chambre funéraire de L. Arruntius

A *Pezzo di Basso rilievo di Stucco in forma più grande, situato nel centro della Volta della Camera. Egli rappresenta senza dubbio un Fatto, ea'avventura quello di Orizia, rapita da Borea, per quanto da questi rotti avanzi si può congetturare, ed ancora dal panno agitato per aria, dall'impeto dello stesso Vento.* B *Lucerne decorate di creta finissima, ritrovate in alcune Celle cinerarie. Sono queste gentilmente lavorate, ed abbellite di vaghi ornamenti, vedendovisi ghirlande, delfini, un putto, che va a caccia de'cani, e la faretra, agli omeri, foglie e grappoli d'uva, ed altre graziose invenzioni.* C *Figura parimente di Stucco nei compartimenti delle pareti della Camera. Stan-* ...*da quella Donna inginocchiata, sembra aver posata a terra una canistra, ed altre canistrelle, ed attendere al ministero della sacra mensa, la quale apparisce esser-* ...*la nelle figure delle Tavole seguenti.* D *Donna, o Sacerdotessa negli Stucchi della Volta, in atto di porgere, o di levare qualche frutto, ed altre cose sopra la mensa, chele sta dinanzi, come vedrassi negli altri pezzi delle Tavole in appresso.*

Iscrizioni e Frammenti delle Camere sepolcrali della Famiglia Arrunzia...
390 x 475 mm

Inscriptions and fragments from the tomb chambers
Inschriften und Fragmente aus den Grabkammern
Inscriptions et fragments des chambres funéraires

...due Colonne co'loro Capitelli, Architrave, Fregio, e Cornice...
348 x 252 mm

Architectural details
Architekturdetails
Détails architecturaux

Grand'Urna di Porfido...
445 x 655 mm

Large porphyry sarcophagus
Großer Porphyrsarkophag
Grand sarcophage en porphyre

Spaccato per traverso della grand Urna ...
545 x 395 mm

Section of the preceding sarcophagus
Aufriß des großen Sarkophags
Coupe du sarcophage précédent

**Veduta degli Avanzi di
Fabbrica magnifica
sepolcrale**
470 x 525 mm

Remains of a
magnificent sepulchral
building

Überreste eines
prachtvollen
Grabgebäudes

Vestiges d'un édifice
funéraire grandiose

VEDUTA degli Avanzi di Fabbrica magnifica sepolcrale
fu

...ue Rovine, la quale si vede vicina a Torre de'Schiavi un miglio e mezzo in circa
di Porta Maggiore

Piranesi Archit. dis. et inc.

VEDUTA di un Sepolcro fuori di Porta del Popolo sull'antica Via Cassia, cinque miglia lontano da Roma; chiamato dal Volgo il Sepolcro di Nerone. Tanto il Sarcofago col suo Coperchio di marmo di rosso antico, quanto i grossi Pezzi di Tufi, e l'altre Pietre, i quali si veggono, gisano uni d'intorno. Anno a contorno, ch' così sia fatto un superbo Mausoleo. Le Sculture però del Sarcofago, sono di mediocre Scalpello, come le due Figure a lato all'Iscrizione in piedi di Castore e Polluce; ovvero di Mylanedro, che dona il Buccefalo; le due Vittorie alati in atto di appendere due Trofei militari, scolpite verso gli angoli del gran Coperchio. Alli sopra messo fora l'Aquile, che tenero sù Scogi, ò Huomo armato, con asta e fondo in mano; nel lato del Coperchio sporche. Il Grifo poi nel lato del Sarcofago, che tiene il Toro, che gli sta sotto, rilevanti un metro dai su fondo, sembrano essere le principali d'ordinario Scalpere. Ma questi Bassorilievi cosi conserved, signati A., nella Base dell'Urna sono ribasso puerili, i pomidei, viridari, che figlio sono prefissi in le pedale viridi Villini.   Piranesi delin. scol. fec.

Veduta di un Sepolcro fuori di Porta del Popolo sull'antica Via Cassia
570 x 395 mm

View of a tomb on the ancient Via Cassia
Ansicht eines Grabes an der alten Via Cassia
Vue d'un tombeau situé sur la via Cassia

VEDUTA di un gran Masso, Avanzo del Sepolcro della Famiglia de' Metelli sulla Via Appia, cinque miglia in circa fuori di Porta S. Sebastiano nel Casale di S. Maria Nuova. Questo nobile Sepolcro fu decorato non solamente de' luci più magnifici ornamenti, ma ancora di vari altre marmi, che le coprira, e fu talmente lavorato all'interno nella parte di sotto pedestrica, che sembra marestile a vedere come possa sussistere quasi affisso per aria una mole si grande. A Avanzo di muro reticolato, il quale può credersi, che servisse di recinto alla Villa de' Metelli, dentro la quale era fabbricato il Sepolcro, accioché celle monte culti dette. B Altri Avanzi de' Sepolcri.

Veduta di un gran Masso, Avanzo del Sepolcro della Famiglia de'Metelli sulla Via Appia
410 x 470 mm

Remains of the tomb of the Metelli
Überreste des Grabes der Metelli
Vestiges du tombeau des Metelli

M·VALERIVS·MESSALLA·CORVINVS
P·RVTILIVS·LVPVS·L·IVNIVS·SILANVS
L·PONTIVS·MELA·D·MARIVS
NIGER·HEREDES·C·CESTI·ET
L·CESTIVS·QVAE·EX·PARTE·AD
EVM·FRATRIS·HEREDITAS
M·AGRIPPAE·MVNERE·PER
VENIT·EX·EA·PECVNIA·QVAM
PRO·SVIS·PARTIBVS·RECEPER
EX·VENDITIONE·ATTALICOR
QVAE·EIS·PER·EDICTVM·AEDILIS
IN·SEPVLCRVM·C·CESTI·EX
TESTAMENTO·EIVS·INFERRE
NON·LICVIT

A *Uno delli due Dadi fatti a guisa di Piedestallo in tutto simili, i quali esistono nel Museo Capitolino, trovati in tempo di Aleßandro VII nelle scavi, che si fece allora d'intorno alla Piramide.* B *Piramide di una Statua colosale di metallo ivi presso ritrovati.* C *Basamento di Travertino composto di due vori a foggia di Scoglio sopra il quale posa la Piramide. Giace ora sotto il terreno.* D *Frammenti di colonne doriche delle Basi, e di un Basamento sotto alle medesime ritrovate lo stato nella maniera, che si vede presentesi.* E *Capitelli voluti in vari aspetti dispersi qua e là, più grandi di quelli delle Colonne, aßieche insieme a tutti insino le parti loro.* F *Colonne formate di Pidstetti formati, d'innalzato nel tempo del* *ristauro della Piramide.* G *Veduta della facciata della Piramide dalla parte di Ponente.* H *Mura di Roma.*

Piranesi Archit. dis. et inc.

Uno delli due Dadi fatti a guisa di Piedestallo in tutto simili, i quali esistono nel Museo Capitolino...
505 x 393 mm

One of two identical pedestals in the Capitoline Museum
Einer der zwei Piedestale im Kapitolinischen Museum
Un des deux piédestaux conservés au musée Capitolin

...Tomo quarto contenente i ponti antichi, gli avanzi de'teatri, de'portici...
400 x 253 mm

Title page to Vol. IV, containing bridges, remains of theaters and arcades
Titelblatt zu Bd. IV, der antike Brücken, Überreste von Theatern und Säulengängen beinhaltet
Page de titre du vol. IV : Ponts antiques, vestiges de théâtres et de portiques

Tom. IV.

B

E

C

D

A

VEDUTA di un Ingresso alla Stanza superiore dentro al Masso sepolcrale d'Elio Adriano Imp. A Stipite formato in parte dai Cunei di Travertino, i quali compongono il grand
Arco, come riempitura. Questo grand'Arco maravigliosam.^{te} rinforzato ne'suoi lati quanto di resistenza fa al gravissimo peso del Masso, postogli sopra, altrettante solleva le
C Linea, la quale dimostra la Volta degli Anditi, descritti nelle Tav. antecedenti. D Spazio, o sia Porzione de'suddi Cunei, la quale vista scoperta sotto la Volta medesima degli A
niun'alta impressione di straordinaria gravita, e sodezza; la quale, si puo dire, che non cede punto a quella delle rinomate Piramidi d'Egitto. E Bozze, le quali sorivano per at
F Stanza con Volta a botte, ricoperta di moderna intonicatura. G L'altro Ingresso, o Porta simile alla descritta.

Veduta di un Ingresso alla Stanza Superiore dentro al Masso sepolcrale d'Elio Adriano Imp.^re
365 x 475 mm

Entrance to the upper room inside the mausoleum

Eingang zum oberen Raum des Mausoleums

Entrée pour accéder à la pièce la plus haute du mausolée

Della Magnificenza ed Architettura de'Romani, Opera di Gio. Battista Piranesi, socio della reale accademia degli antiquarj di Londra

Edition Rome 1761. Title engraved on the second title page: *On the Grandeur and the Architecture of the Romans by Gio. Battista Piranesi, Fellow of the Royal Society of Antiquaries of London.* The volume consists of 2 title pages (Latin, Italian), portrait of Clement XIII, 3 ornamented letters, 2 vignettes, plates numbered I–XXXVIII, Italian and Latin text. Plate XXX, *Section of the Emissarium at Lake Albano*, is analogous to Plate III of the *Descrizione dell'Emissario del Lago di Albano*.

Editions Paris. With the addition of the pamphlets: *Observations of Giovanni Battista Piranesi on the letter of M. Mariette; Opinions on the Architecture, Treatise on the introduction and the progress of the Fine Arts*. Plates numbered from 285 to 330. Except for the text ornaments, the copperplates are preserved at the Calcografia in Rome (vol. VII).
Preparation of the book and execution of the plates may have started a few years before publication. Critical references go back to the years 1755–58. The printing permit is dated 1760, while the delay in its publication was due to the time needed to complete the Pope's portrait.
In the order of the plates kept at the Calcografia, which corresponds to the Firmin Didot

Ausgabe Rom 1761. Der italienische Titel ist in das zweite Titelblatt gestochen: *Über die Großartigkeit und die Architektur der Römer, Werk des Gio. Battista Piranesi, Mitglied der Königlichen Akademie der Antiquare von London.* 2 Titelblätter (lateinisch, italienisch), Porträt von Papst Klemens XIII., 3 Initialen, 2 Vignetten, Tafeln I–XXXVIII numeriert, ein italienischer und ein lateinischer Text. Die Tafel XXX stimmt mit der Tafel III der *Descrizione dell'Emissario del Lago di Albano* überein.

Ausgaben Paris. Hinzufügung der Pamphlete: *Anmerkungen über den Brief von M. Mariette; Über die Architektur; Einführung und zu der Entwicklung der Schönen Künste.*
Die Vorbereitung für das Buch und die Ausführung der Druckplatten dürften einige Jahre vor der Herausgabe begonnen haben, die polemischen Anspielungen reichen bis in die Jahre 1755–1758 zurück. Die Publikationslizenz ist 1760 datiert. Die Verzögerung bei der Veröffentlichung erklärt sich durch die Fertigstellung des Papstporträts. Die Tafeln sind von 285 bis 300 numeriert. Mit Ausnahme der Textornamente werden die Platten in der Calcografia in Rom aufbewahrt (Band VII).

Edition de Rome 1761. Titre gravé en italien sur le deuxième frontispice : *De la Grandeur et de l'Architecture des Romains. Œuvre de Gio. Battista Piranesi, membre de la Société royale des antiquaires de Londres.* L'ouvrage a deux frontispices (latin et italien), un portrait de Clément XIII, trois lettres ornées, deux vignettes, les planches I à XXXVIII et un texte italien et latin. La planche XXX, *Coupe de l'Emissario au lac d'Albano*, est similaire à la planche III de la *Descrizione dell'Emissario del Lago di Albano*.

Editions de Paris. Ajout des opuscules : *Observations sur la lettre de M. Mariette ; Opinions sur l'architecture ; Introduction sur les progrès des beaux-arts.* Planches numérotées de 285 à 330. Exceptés les motifs ornementaux du texte, les cuivres sont conservés à la Chalcographie de Rome (tome VII).
La préparation du livre et la réalisation des matrices a dû commencer quelques années avant l'impression : les références à diverses polémiques concernent les années 1755–58. Le permis d'imprimer est de 1760, le retard à l'impression s'explique par le délai supplémentaire pour le portrait du Pape ; la date de l'édition est gravée dans la planche du titre latin. Dans le classement du fonds de matrices de la

edition, the following plates are found between plate XVI and plate XX: 302 without Roman numeral; 303 with number XVII; 307 changed to 304, with Roman numeral XIX changed by hand to XVIIa; 305 without Roman numeral; 306 with Roman numeral XVIII; 307 with Roman numeral XIX.

In der Reihenfolge der Platten in der Calcografia, die mit derjenigen der Ausgabe von Firmin Didot übereinstimmt, finden sich zwischen den Tafeln XVI und XX folgende Tafeln: 302 ohne römische Numerierung, 303 mit der Nummer XVII, 307 verbessert in 304, mit der römischen Nummer XIX per Hand in XVIIa korrigiert, 305 ohne römische Nummer, 306 mit der römischen Nummer XVIII und 307 mit der römischen Nummer XIX.

Chalcographie, qui correspond à l'édition Firmin Didot, entre la planche XVI et la planche XX se trouvent les planches suivantes : 302 sans n° romain, 303 avec le n° romain XVII, 307 changé en 304, avec le n° romain XIX corrigé à la main en XVIIa, 305 sans n° romain, 306 avec le n° romain XVIII et 307 avec le n° romain XIX.

... De romanorum magnificentia et architectura
428 x 318 mm

First title page (Latin text):
On the Grandeur and the Architecture of the Romans
Erstes Titelblatt (lateinischer Text):
Über die Größe und die Architektur der Römer
Première page de titre (texte latin) :
De la Grandeur et de l'Architecture des Romains

Variae in Architectura graecanica rationes …
600 x 395 mm

Various Greek columns taken from ancient monuments
Verschiedene Säulen griechischer Architektur
Différentes colonnes grecques provenant de monuments antiques

Column bases
compared with
illustrations from
Le Roy

Säulenbasen im
Vergleich mit
Abbildungen von
Le Roy

Bases de colonne
comparées avec des
planches de Le Roy

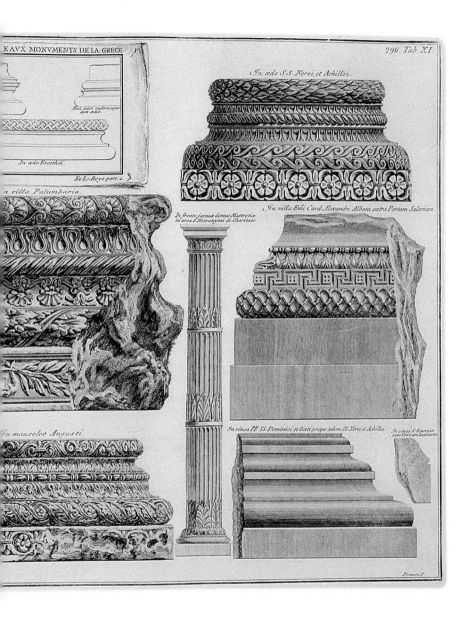

Deli inter rudera cujus dam ædis.

In æde Erecthei.

Ex Lo. Reyo part. 2.

In æde S.S. Nerei, et Achillei.

In villa Palumbaria

In fronte januæ domus Mastrotti in area S. Hieronymi de Charitate

In villa Emi Card. Alexandri Albani extra Portam Salariam.

In mausoleo Augusti.

In vinea PP. SS. Dominici et Sixti prope ædem SS Nerei et Achillei.

In vinea S. Joannis ante Portam Latinam.

Piranesi F.

In villa Alteria.

In hortis Palatinis Farnesianis

In domo Verospia.

In vestibulo ædis Divi Xisti prope
Thermas Antoninianas

In villa Palumbaria.

Ad Suburram novam penes Lapicidinam
prope imaginem SS. Crucifixi.

In villa Strotia.

In villa Barbarinorum prope Albam.

Transtyberim in ædibus Farnesianis

Transtyberim in ædibus Farnesianis

In ædibus Farnesianis ubi visitur symplegn

In villa Negronia

299 Tab XIV

Ante ædem SS. Nerei et Achillei

In villa Alteria

In villa Casali

In villa Barbarinorum prope Albam

Cæsi Candul in dorso lib. Cuccomos

Ante januam villa Altoria

[Vari capitelli e bassorilievi]
410 x 675 mm

Various capitals and bas-reliefs

Verschiedene Kapitelle und Basreliefs

Divers chapiteaux et bas-reliefs

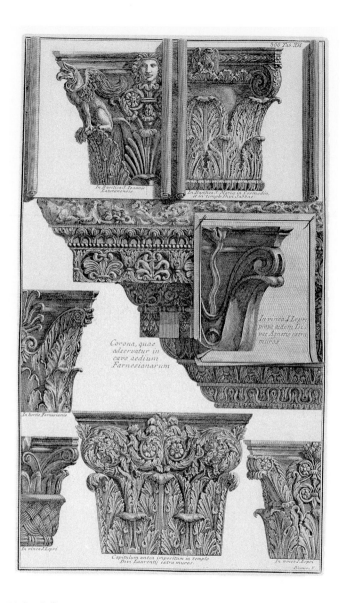

[Vari capitelli]
470 x 275 mm

Various capitals
Verschiedene Kapitelle
Divers chapiteaux

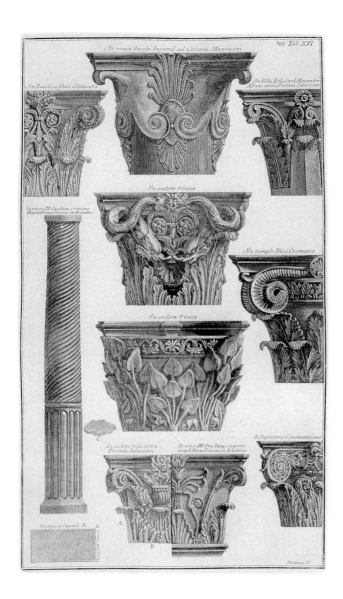

[Vari capitelli ed una colonna]
460 x 270 mm

Various capitals and a column
Verschiedene Kapitelle und eine Säule
Divers chapiteaux et une colonne

Il Campo Marzio dell'Antica Roma, Opera di G. B. Piranesi socio della reale società degli antiquari di Londra

Edition Rome 1762. Engraved title on the title page: *The Campus Martius of Ancient Rome, the Work of G. B. Piranesi, Fellow of the Royal Society of Antiquaries, London.* The Latin title page bears the title, the date of the edition, and the dedication to Robert Adam. The address is: "Veneunt apud Auctorem in aedibus Comitis Thomati via Felice prope Templum SS. Trinitatis in Monte Pincio". The volume is composed of 2 title pages (Latin and Italian, whose sequence varies according to the copy), 2 ornamented letters, 4 vignettes, 42 plates by Piranesi (5 of these plates are composed of several copperplates), and 1 engraved by Vesterhout, 68 pages of text in Italian and Latin, preceded by 6 pages of dedication to Robert Adam and followed by 29 pages of indices.

Editions Paris: the plates are numbered from 418 to 455. Except for the text ornaments, the copperplates are preserved at the Calcografia in Rome (vol. X). The genesis of the work goes back to the second half of the 1750s: its publication is announced as imminent in the first volume of *Antichità Romane* (1756). The large Plan of Campo Marzio in 6 copperplates (*"Ichnographia" or plan of the Campus*

Ausgabe Rom 1762. Der italienische Titel ist in das Titelblatt gestochen: *Der Campus Martius des Antiken Rom, Werk des G. B. Piranesi, Mitglied der Königlichen Gesellschaft der Antiquare von London.* Lateinisches Titelblatt mit Titel, Erscheinungsjahr und Widmung an Robert Adam. Die Adresse lautet: „Veneunt apud Auctorem in aedibus Comitis Thomati via Felice prope Templum SS. Ttinitatis in Monte Pincio". Der Band enthält: 2 Titelblätter (lateinisch und italienisch; die Reihenfolge variiert in den einzelnen Exemplaren), 2 Initialen, 4 Vignetten, 42 Tafeln von Piranesi (fünf dieser Tafeln setzen sich aus mehreren Platten zusammen), eine von Westerhout gestochene Tafel, Widmungstext an Robert Adam (6 Seiten), italienischer und lateinischer Text (68 Seiten), Inhaltsverzeichnis (29 Seiten).

Ausgaben Paris: Die Tafeln sind von 418 bis 455 numeriert. Mit Ausnahme der Textornamente werden die Platten in der Calcografia in Rom aufbewahrt (Band X). Die Entstehung des Werkes reicht in die zweite Hälfte der fünfziger Jahre des 18. Jahrhunderts zurück; seine Veröffentlichung wird bereits im ersten Band der *Antichità Romane* 1756

Edition de Rome 1762. Titre italien gravé sur le frontispice : *Le Champ de Mars de la Rome antique. Œuvre de G. B. Piranesi, membre de la Société royale des antiquaires de Londres.* Le frontispice latin porte le titre, la date de l'édition et la dédicace à Robert Adam. L'adresse est : « Veneunt apud Auctorem in aedibus Comitis Thomati via Felice prope Templum SS. Ttinitatis in Monte Pincio. » L'ouvrage est composé de deux frontispices (latin et italien dont l'ordre varie selon les différents exemplaires), de deux lettres ornées, de quatre vignettes, de 42 planches de Piranesi (cinq d'entre elles sont composées de plusieurs cuivres), et d'une planche gravée par Vesterhout. Le texte comprend 68 pages, en italien et en latin, il est précédé de six pages de dédicace à Robert Adam et suivi de 29 pages d'index.

Editions de Paris : Les planches sont numérotées de 418 à 455. A l'exception des motifs ornementaux du texte, les cuivres sont conservés à la Chalcographie de Rome (tome X). L'origine de l'œuvre remonte à la seconde moitié des années 1750, sa publication est annoncée comme imminente dans le premier tome des *Antichità Romane* (1756). Le grand plan du

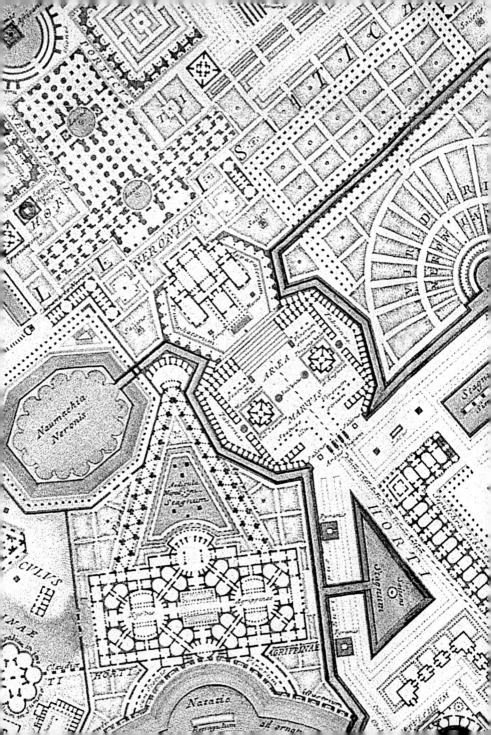

Martius, ill. p. 95), executed in collaboration with Robert Adam and dedicated to him, is dated 1757 on the plate. The *approbatio* is dated 1761. The plate by Vesterhout (plate XXXI, not illustrated here) reproduces the technical solution adopted by Carlo and Francesco Fontana for restoration of the Column of Antoninus Pius in 1705.

angekündigt. Der große Plan des Campus Martius auf sechs Platten (Abb. S. 95), der in Zusammenarbeit mit Robert Adam entstand und diesem gewidmet wurde, ist in der Platte 1757 datiert. Die Publikationslizenz ist 1761 datiert. Die Platte von Westerhout (Tafel XXXI, hier nicht abgebildet) gibt die von Carlo und Francesco Fontana angewandte technische Lösung zur Wiederaufrichtung der Säule des Antoninus Pius im Jahre 1705 wieder.

Champ de Mars en six cuivres, « *Ichnographia* » *ou plan du Champ de Mars* (p. 95) réalisé en collaboration avec Robert Adam et qui lui est dédicacé est daté, sur la pierre, 1757. L'approbation remonte à 1761. La plaque de Vesterhout (planche XXXI, non représentée ici) reproduit la solution technique adoptée par Carlo et Francesco Fontana pour la remise en état de la colonne d'Antonin le Pieux en 1705.

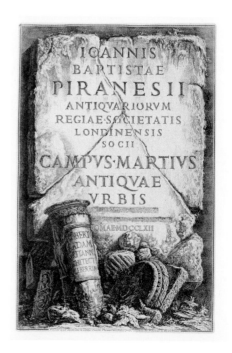

Ioannis Baptistae Piranesii [...] Campus Martius Antiquae Urbis ...
500 x 335 mm

Title page: The Campus Martius of the Ancient City
Titelblatt: Der Campus Martius der antiken Stadt
Page de titre : Le Champ de Mars de la Ville antique

Ichnographiam Campi Martii antiquae urbis
1350 x 1170 mm

"Ichnographia" or plan of the Campus Martius
„Ichnographia" oder Plan des Campus Martius
«Ichnographia» ou plan du Champ de Mars

Ichnographia vicinae reliquiarum Theatri Pompejani
365 × 235 mm

Map of the neighborhood of the theater of Pompey
Karte der Umgebung des Pompejus-Theaters
Carte de la zone voisine du théâtre de Pompée

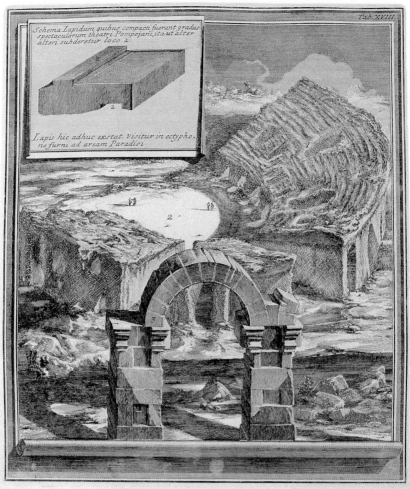

Reliquiae Theatri Pompejani

1. Substructiones graduum spectaculorum, quorum forma in efficta tabella demon-stratur. 2. Orchestra. 3. Arcus residuus substructionum theatri

Vide indicem ruinarum num. 54. *Piranesi F.*

Reliquiae Theatri Pompejani
280 x 250 mm

Remains of the theater of Pompey
Überreste des Pompejus-Theaters
Vestiges du théâtre de Pompée

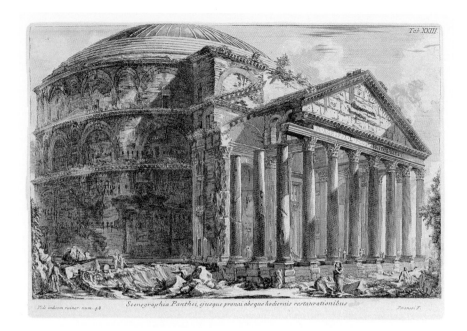

Tab. XXIII

Vide indicem ruinar: num. 43   Scenographia Panthei, ejusque pronai absque hodiernis restaurationibus   Piranesi F.

Scenographia Panthei, ejusque pronai...
225 x 350 mm

View of the Pantheon and its entrance
Ansicht des Pantheons und des Pronaos
Vue du Panthéon et du pronaos

Tab. XXVII.

Reliquiae theatri Marcelli. A. *Rudera porticus retro scenam ipsius theatri.*
B *Ruinæ substructionum graduum spectaculorum.*
Vide indicem ruinarum num. 62.

Piranesi F.

Reliquiae theatri Marcelli
232 x 350 mm

Remains of the theater of Marcellus
Überreste des Marcellus-Theaters
Vestiges du théâtre de Marcellus

A. et B. Orthographia utriusque lateris arcuum ductus Aquae Virginis…
340 x 205 mm

Elevation of the arches of the Acqua Vergine
Aufriß der Bögen der Acqua Vergine
Elévation des arches de l'Acqua Vergine

Tab. XXXIII.

C. *Latus Stylobatae columnae apotheoseos Antonini Pii, et Faustinae, posticum lateri A praecedentis tabulae.* D. *Alterum Latus, posticum Lateri B, in praecedente tabula item demonstrato, dexterumque Lateri C.* E. *Tessellae recens factae ad resarciendum Stylobatam.*
Piranesi F.

Latus Stylobatae columnae apotheoseos Antonini Pii, et Faustinae...
340 x 280 mm

Base of the column of Antoninus Pius
Basis der Antoninus-Pius-Säule
Base de la colonne d'Antonin le Pieux

Tab XXXVI

Arcus Marci Aurelij Imp. ex ejus archetypis efformatis antequam destrueretur ob ampliandum hippodromum A, B Anaglyphi qui asservantur in aedibus Capitolinis C Columna Cochliodes ejusdem Marci.

Arcus Marci Aurelii Imp ...
360 x 235 mm

Arch of the emperor Marcus Aurelius
Bogen des Kaisers Mark Aurel
L'arc de Marc Aurèle

Interiora Balnearum Sallustianarum

Piranesi F.

Interiora Balnearum Sallustianarum
260 x 292 mm

Interior of the baths of Sallust
Innenansicht der Sallust-Thermen
Intérieur des thermes de Salluste

Tab. XXXVIII.

1. *Rudera viae Flaminiae.* 2. *Solum viae ab imbribus praeruptum.* 3. *Silices, et* 4. *glarea, quibus via antiquitus muniebatur.* 5. *Iter novum.*
Vide indicem ruinar. num. 6. 7.

Piranesi F.

Rudera viae Flaminiae
220 x 350 mm

Remains of the Via Flaminia
Überreste der Via Flaminia
Vestiges de la via Flaminia

Elevazione del Pantheon, e degli altri edifizi che gli eran vicini.

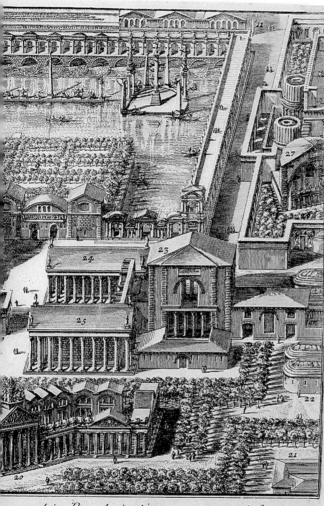

graphia Panthei aliorumque aedificiorum,
e prope habuit.

Piranesi F.

Elevazione del
Pantheon, e degli altri
edifizi che gli eran vicini
170 x 287 mm

View of the Pantheon
and the other buildings
in its vicinity

Ansicht des Pantheons
und benachbarter
Bauten

Elévation du Panthéon
et des édifices voisins

Descrizione e Disegno dell'Emissario del Lago Albano di Gio Battista Piranesi

Edition Rome 1762. Title engraved on the title page: *Description and Design of the Emissarium of Lake Albano by Gio. Battista Piranesi*. Volume composed of a title page, an ornamented letter, a tail piece, 9 plates and 20 pages of text. In the appendix: *Di due spelonche ornate dagli antichi alla riva del lago Albano* (printed title), edition composed of a vignette and 9 plates; 9 plates of text, 12 plates.

Editions Paris: the plates are numbered from 484 to 494 and from 495 to 504; two of the plates of the original edition are in two parts. Except for the text ornaments, the copperplates are preserved at the Calcografia in Rome (vol. XI, parts II–III). The date of the edition may be inferred from the *approbatio* of the *Descrizione* (April 1, 1762), and the date given in the appendix (August 30, 1762). It frequently occurs that the *Descrizione* and its appendix are bound together with the *Antichità di Albano e di Castel Gandolfo* of 1764, and thus they are often considered a single edition starting with the states of the engraved *Catalogo* that appeared after 1764. They are also combined in a single volume (XI) in the Firmin Didot arrangement.

Ausgabe Rom 1762. Titel in das Titelblatt gestochen: *Beschreibung und Zeichnung des Entwässerungskanals des Albaner Sees von Gio. Battista Piranesi*. Der Band enthält: Titelblatt, Initiale, Schlußvignette, 9 Tafeln und 20 Textseiten. Im Anhang: *Di due spelonche ornate dagli antichi alla riva del lago Albano* (gedruckter Titel), die Ausgabe enthält eine Vignette, 9 Tafeln, 9 Textseiten, 12 Tafeln.

Ausgaben Paris: Die Tafeln sind von 484 bis 494 und von 495 bis 504 numeriert; 2 Tafeln der Originalausgabe sind in zwei Teilen ausgeführt. Mit Ausnahme der Textornamente werden die Platten in der Calcografia in Rom aufbewahrt (Band XI, Teile II und III). Das Erscheinungsjahr der Ausgabe ist der Publikationslizenz der *Descrizione* (1. April 1762) sowie den Angaben im Anhang (30. August 1762) zu entnehmen. Oft ist die *Descrizione* und ihr Anhang mit den *Antichità di Albano e di Castelgandolfo* von 1764 zusammengebunden und wurde daher häufig als eine Ausgabe behandelt, wie bereits in den nach 1764 gestochenen Ausgaben des *Catalogo*. In einem Band (XI) sind sie auch in der Anordnung von Firmin Didot vereinigt.

Edition de Rome 1762. Titre gravé sur le frontispice : *Description et représentation de l'Emissario du lac d'Albano de Gio. Battista Piranesi*. Ouvrage composé d'un frontispice, d'une lettre ornée, d'un cul-de-lampe, de neuf planches et de 20 pages de texte. Appendice : *Di due spelonche ornate dagli antichi alla riva del lago Albano* (titre typographié), édition composée d'une vignette, de douze planches et de neuf planches de texte.

Editions de Paris : Les planches sont numérotées de 484 à 494 et de 495 à 504 ; deux des planches de l'édition originale sont en deux parties. A l'exception des motifs ornementaux du texte, les cuivres sont conservés à la Chalcographie de Rome (tome XI, parties II–III). La date de l'édition peut se déduire de l'approbation de la *Descrizione* (datée 1er avril 1762) et de l'appendice (daté 30 août 1762). Généralement, la *Descrizione* et son appendice étaient reliés avec les *Antichità di Albano e di Castel Gandolfo* de 1764 et furent considérés, dans les tirages successifs du *Catalogo* gravé, comme une seule et même édition. Elles sont également réunies dans le même volume dans le classement effectué par Firmin Didot.

**Dimostrazioni
dell'Emissario del
Lago Albano
450 x 640 mm**

Illustrations of the
emissarium of Lake
Albano

Darstellungen des
Entwässerungskanals
des Albaner Sees

Relevés de l'Emissario
du lac d'Albano

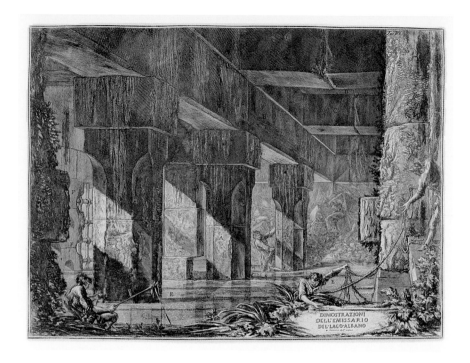

Dimostrazioni dell'Emissario del Lago Albano
410 x 555 mm

Illustrations of the emissarium of Lake Albano
Darstellungen des Entwässerungskanals des Albaner Sees
Relevés de l'Emissario du lac d'Albano

Dimostrazioni dell'Emissario del Lago Albano
410 x 635 mm

Illustrations of the emissarium of Lake Albano
Darstellungen des Entwässerungskanals des Albaner Sees
Relevés de l'Emissario du lac d'Albano

Prospettiva dello stesso Delubro
600 x 910 mm

View of the same sanctuary
Ansicht desselben Heiligtums
Vue du même sanctuaire

Dimostrazione in grande del criptoportico...
183 x 276 mm

Detail of the cryptoporticus
Detail der Kryptoportikus
Détail du cryptoportique

Diverse Maniere d'adornare i cammini ed ogni altra parte degli edifizi desunte dall'architettura Egizia, Etrusca, e Greca con un Ragionamento Apologetico in defesa dell'Architettura Egizia, e Toscana, opera del Cavaliere Giambattista Piranesi architetto

Edition Rome 1769. Printed title: *Divers Ways of ornamenting chimneypieces and all other parts of houses taken from Egyptian, Etruscan, and Grecian architecture with an Apologia in defense of Egyptian and Tuscan architecture, the work of Cavaliere Giambattista Piranesi.* Volume composed of a title page, 67 plates, with 3 vignettes and 3 plates. Printed dedication of 2 pages to Mons. Giovanni Battista Rezzonico; 35 pages of text (Italian, French, English), with a headpiece, tailpiece, vignette, and 3 plates of illustration.

Edition Paris: text in Italian only; title page and plates numbered from 874 to 911. Except for the text ornaments, the copperplates are preserved at the Calcografia dell'Istituto Nazionale per la Grafica, Rome (vol. XX). Preparation of the volume required several years, and the engraving and publication of individual plates began long before the publishing date of the complete edition. As confirmed by documentary evidence, several prints were in circulation before 1767, as well as incomplete test copies of the volume. The sequence of subjects frequently varies between one copy and another of the definitive edition.

Ausgabe Rom 1769: *Verschiedene Arten Kamine zu schmücken und alle anderen Teile der Gebäude, der ägyptischen, etruskischen und griechischen Architektur entnommen, mit einer apologetischen Erörterung zur Verteidigung der ägyptischen und toskanischen Architektur, Werk des Cavaliere Giambattista Piranesi, Architekt.* Der Band enthält: Titelblatt, 67 Tafeln, 3 Vignetten und 3 Tafeln, zweiseitige Widmung an Monsignore Giovanni Battista Rezzonico, 35 Textseiten (italienisch, französisch, englisch) mit 3 Vignetten und 3 Abbildungstafeln.

Ausgabe Paris: Nur der italienische Text, Titelblatt, numerierte Tafeln von 874 bis 911. Mit Ausnahme der Textornamente werden die Platten in der Calcografia in Rom aufbewahrt (Band XX). Die Vorbereitung des Bandes nahm einige Jahre in Anspruch, aber der Druck und die Verbreitung einzelner Tafeln datiert wesentlich früher als das Erscheinungsjahr. Nachweislich waren einige Stiche bereits 1767 in Umlauf, ebenso frühe, unvollständige Probeexemplare der Ausgabe. In der endgültigen Edition variiert die Abfolge der Themen in den verschiedenen Exemplaren.

Edition de Rome 1769. Titre typographié : *Différentes manières d'orner les cheminées et toutes les autres parties de la maison à partir de l'architecture égyptienne, étrusque et grecque suivi d'un Discours en faveur de l'architecture égyptienne et toscane, œuvre du chevalier Giambattista Piranesi.* Ouvrage composé d'un frontispice, de 67 planches, avec trois vignettes et trois planches. Dédicace typographiée de deux pages à Mgr Giovanni Battista Rezzonico ; 35 pages de texte (italien, français, anglais), un en-tête, un bas de page, une vignette et trois planches d'illustrations.

Edition de Paris : Il n'y a que le texte italien, un frontispice et les planches numérotées de 874 à 911. A l'exception des motifs ornementaux du texte, les cuivres sont conservés à la Chalcographie de Rome (tome XX). La préparation du volume a nécessité de nombreuses années et la gravure et la diffusion de planches isolées ont commencé bien avant la date d'édition. Comme l'attestent certains documents, quelques estampes ainsi que des copies d'épreuves incomplètes du volume circulaient déjà dès 1767. Dans l'édition définitive, l'ordre de présentation des différents sujets change fréquemment d'un exemplaire à l'autre.

[Tavola di vasi e di conchiglie]
383 x 252 mm

Shells and vase designs
Muscheln und Vasenentwürfe
Coquillages et modèles de vase

[Diversi monumenti etruschi]
382 x 252 mm

Various Etruscan monuments
Verschiedene etruskische Denkmäler
Divers monuments étrusques

Cammino che si vede nel Palazzo di Sua Ecc.za Milord Conte D'Exeter...
340 x 240 mm

Chimneypiece designed for Lord Exeter
Kaminentwurf für Lord Exeter
Cheminée dessinée pour Lord Exeter

Questo Camino si vede in marmo nel gabinetto di S.E. Il Sig.ʳ Prencipe [...] Rezzonico...
405 x 265 mm

Chimneypiece in the cabinet of Prince Rezzonico
Kamin im Kabinett des Fürsten Rezzonico
Cheminée du cabinet du prince Rezzonico

122

[Camino con figura di
cariatide sui montanti]
240 x 325 mm

Design for a
chimneypiece

Kaminentwurf

Dessin d'une cheminée

[Camino egizio con due grandi figure sorreggenti il fregio]
245 x 380 mm

Design for a chimneypiece in Egyptian style
Kaminentwurf im ägyptisierenden Stil
Dessin d'une cheminée à l'égyptienne

Altro spaccato per longo della stessa bottega, ove si vedono, frà le aperture del vestibolo le immense piramidi, ed altri edifizj sepolerali ne' deserti dell' Egitto.

Disegno ed invenzione del Cavalier Piranesi   Cav. Piranesi F.   95

Altro spaccato per longo della stessa bottega ...
210 x 320 mm

Egyptian decoration of the Caffè degli Inglesi
Ägyptisierende Dekoration für das Caffè degli Inglesi
Décoration de style égyptien pour le Caffè degli Inglesi

[Vari modelli di mobilia tra cui un tavolo con piedi ornati da grifoni]
385 x 252 mm

Clocks and miscellaneous furniture
Uhren und verschiedene Möbelstücke
Pendules et diverses pièces de mobilier

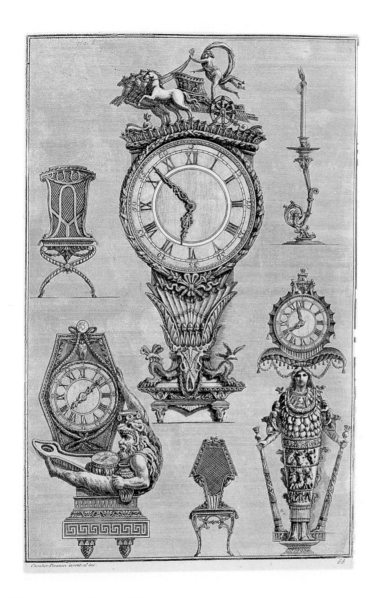

[Tre orologi, due sedie, un candeliere]
375 x 245 mm

Clocks and miscellaneous furniture
Uhren und verschiedene Möbelstücke
Pendules et diverses pièces de mobilier

Vasi, candelabri, cippi, sarcofagi, tripodi, lucerne, ed ornamenti antichi disegnati ed incisi dal Cav. Gio. Batt. Piranesi pubblicati l'anno MDCCLXXIIX

Edition Rome 1778. Title engraved on the title page: *Vases, candelabra, grave stones, sarcophagi, tripods, lamps, and ornaments designed and etched by Cav. Gio. Batt. Piranesi, published in the year 1778*, 2 volumes.

Editions Paris: the plates are numbered from 505 to 618. The copperplates are preserved at the Calcografia in Rome (vol. XII–XIII).
The series, which was probably executed in its entirety by Giovanni Battista's son Francesco and his school on the basis of drawings by Giovanni Battista, was continued by Francesco after his father's death. Giovanni Battista worked on it from 1768 to 1778. The plates first appeared separately, and were later combined in collections of various sizes; the best-known ones contain 110 plates plus the 2 title pages in an edition that was probably edited by Francesco, through not before 1779, and only from that time on sold in complete form.

Ausgabe Rom 1778. Titel in das Titelblatt gestochen: *Vasen, Kandelaber, Urnen, Sarkophage, Dreifüße, Lampen und antike Ornamente gezeichnet und gestochen von Cav. Gio. Batt. Piranesi, publiziert im Jahr 1778*, 2 Bände.

Ausgaben Paris: Die Tafeln sind von 505 bis 618 numeriert. Die Druckplatten werden in der Calcografia in Rom aufbewahrt.
Die vermutlich komplett von dem Sohn und der Werkstatt nach Zeichnungen von Giovanni Battista ausgeführte Folge wurde von Francesco Piranesi nach dem Tod seines Vaters fortgeführt. Giovanni Battista arbeitete an ihr zwischen 1768 und 1778. Die Tafeln erschienen zunächst einzeln und wurden erst später in Konvoluten unterschiedlichen Umfangs zusammengestellt. Die bekanntesten umfassen 110 Tafeln und 2 Titelblätter. Für diese Ausgabe zeichnete offenbar Francesco Piranesi verantwortlich; sie ist nicht vor 1779 entstanden und wurde erst dann in dieser vollständigen Form in den Handel gebracht.

Edition de Rome 1778. Titre gravé sur le frontispice : *Vases, candélabres, cippes, sarcophages, tripodes, lampes et ornements antiques dessinés et gravés par le Cav. Gio. Batt. Piranesi publiés l'an 1778*, deux tomes.

Editions de Paris : Les planches sont numérotées de 505 à 618. Les cuivres sont conservés à la Chalcographie de Rome (tomes XII et XIII).
La série probablement exécutée par le fils et l'atelier d'après des dessins de Giovanni Battista fut continuée par Francesco à la mort de son père. Celui-ci y travailla de 1768 à 1778. Les planches parurent d'abord séparément puis furent réunies en recueils d'importance inégale. Les recueils les plus connus comptent 110 planches plus les deux frontispices dans une édition réalisée par Francesco certainement vers 1779 et vendue alors comme un ensemble.

Veduta in Prospettiva di un antico Vaso di marmo...
720 x 475 mm

Large antique vase of marble known as "Warwick Vase"
Große antike Marmorvase, „Warwick Vase" genannt
Grand vase antique en marbre, dit «vase Warwick»

Vaso Cinerario Antico di Marmo ornato a guisa di un Capitello Corintio con Frondi, Delfini, e
Caulicoli di ottima Scultura. Nell'altra Facciata si legge un'Iscrizione della Persona, le cui Ceneri
combuste sono state in esso riposte. Si vede nel Gabinetto di Sua Ecc. il Sig. Principe Altieri

Veduta di fianco dello stesso Vaso.

[Due vedute di vaso cinerario dalla collezione Altieri]
392 x 252 mm

Two views of a cinerary vase
Zwei Ansichten einer Grabvase
Deux vues d'un vase funéraire

Lucerne antiche di Bronzo...
380 x 530 mm

Various lamps of bronze
Verschiedene Bronzelampen
Diverses lampes en bronze

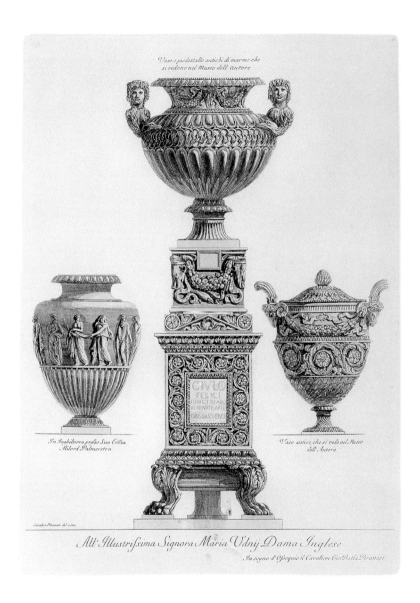

Vaso e piedestallo antichi di marmo che
si vedono nel Museo dell'autore

GIVLO
FELICI
DEMETRIANO
MARMORARIO
ORDINIS SVI SVM

In Inghilterra presso Sua Ecc.za
Milord Palmerston

Vaso antico, che si vede nel Museo
dell'Autore

Cavalier Piranesi del'e inc.

All'Illustrissima Signora Maria Vdnij Dama Inglese

In segno d'Ossequio il Cavaliere Gio.Batta Piranesi

[Tre vasi con un piedistallo antico]
530 x 388 mm

Three vases and an antique pedestal
Drei Vasen und ein antikes Piedestal
Trois vases et un piédestal antique

Altare antico di marmo ritrovato fra le macerie della Villa Adriana nel sito detto Pantanello
530 x 385 mm

Marble altar found in Hadrian's villa
Antiker Marmoraltar, in der Hadriansvilla gefunden
Autel antique en marbre retrouvé à la villa Adriana

Tripode antico di Bronzo che si conserva à Portici "
nel Museo Reale di Sua Maestà Il Rè delle due Sicilie

Al Signor Cavaliere Roberto Smyth Inglese
amatore delle belle arti
In atto di ossequio il Cavaliere Gio Batta Piranesi D.D.D.

Piranesi Fecchio Incepse   Cavalier Piranesi inc.

Tripode antico di Bronzo che si conserva a Portici nel Museo Reale...
530 x 385 mm

Antique bronze tripod in the Royal Museum at Portici
Antiker Bronzedreifuß im Königlichen Museum von Portici
Tripode antique en bronze du musée royal de Portici

Urna Cineraria antica di marmo con suo coperchio...
390 x 255 mm

Cinerary urn with lid
Antike Aschenurne aus Marmor mit Deckel
Urne funéraire en marbre avec couvercle

[Vari candelabri, un vaso e due urne cinerarie]
535 × 430 mm

Three candelabra, a vase and two cinerary urns
Drei Kandelaber, eine Vase und zwei Aschenurnen
Trois candélabres, un vase et deux urnes funéraires

Monumento antico ritrovato fra le ruine di un Sepolcro sulla Via Appia...
535 x 390 mm

Antique monument found in a tomb on the Via Appia
Monument, in einem Grab an der Via Appia gefunden
Monument retrouvé dans un tombeau sur la via Appia

Profilo di una Nave antica di marmo...
652 x 415 mm

Profile of an antique marble galley
Ansicht eines antiken Marmorschiffs
Navire antique en marbre vu de profil

[Différentes vues de Pesto]
Différentes vues de quelques Restes de trois grands Edifices qui subsistent encore dans le milieu de l'ancienne Ville de Pesto autrement dit Posidonia qui est située dans la Lucanie

Edition Rome 1778. Title engraved on title page: *Different views of some of the remains of three great edifices that still exist at the center of the ancient city of Pesto, or Posidonia [Paestum], which is situated in Lucania.* Volume composed of 20 plates in addition to the title plate.

Editions Paris: the plates are numbered 661–681.
The title page and plates XIX and XX bear the signature of Francesco Piranesi. The figures for the entire series were executed by the school, particularly by Francesco. The *approbatio* bears the date September 15, 1778; only a few weeks later Giovanni Battista died on November 9, 1778.

Ausgabe Rom 1778; Titel in das Titelblatt gestochen: *Verschiedene Ansichten einiger Ruinen von drei großen noch existierenden Gebäuden des Zentrums der ehemaligen Stadt Pesto oder Posidonia [Paestum] in Lucania.* Der Band enthält: Titelblatt und 20 Tafeln.

Ausgaben Paris: Die Tafeln sind von 661 bis 681 numeriert.
Das Titelblatt sowie die Tafeln XIX und XX sind von Francesco Piranesi signiert.
Die Tafeln der gesamten Folge wurden von der Werkstatt Piranesi, vor allem von seinem Sohn Francesco, ausgeführt.
Die Publikationslizenz trägt das Datum 15. September 1778; wenige Wochen später, am 9. November 1778, starb Giovanni Battista Piranesi.

Edition de Rome 1778. Titre gravé sur le frontispice : *Différentes vues de quelques restes de trois grands édifices qui subsistent encore dans le milieu de l'ancienne ville de Pesto autrement dit Posidonia [Paestum] qui est située dans la Lucanie.* Ouvrage composé de 20 planches en plus du frontispice.

Editions de Paris. Les planches sont numérotées de 661 à 681.
Le frontispice et les planches XIX et XX sont signées par Francesco Piranesi. Les personnages de la série entière ont été réalisés par l'atelier et plus particulièrement par Francesco.
L'approbation porte la date du 15 septembre 1778. Giovanni Battista meurt le 9 novembre de la même année.

Vue des restes intérieurs du Temple de Neptune
445 x 670 mm

Frontispice: View showing the remains of the interior of the temple of Neptune

Frontispiz: Innenansicht der Überreste des Neptun-Tempels

Frontispice : Vue intérieure des vestiges du temple de Neptune

Vüe des restes intérieurs du Temple de Neptune. Nous ne nous etendrons pas à donner un détail l...
d'en presenter un grand apparceil uni a à autres amas de ruines que nous donnerons à aprés dans les Planches. Les V...
Grece, et que sans se donner la peine, et la fatigue de longs voyages, ceux ci peuvent suffire pour contenter la ...

orceaux, parce qu'ils seront bien détaillés, et bien spécifiés dans les Planches suivantes. Dans ce Frontispice nous les avons dessinés tel qu'ils existent aftin
nous assurent que par rapport à l'Architecture Grecque des Temples bâtis dans l'Ordre Dorique, ceux de Pesto sont superieurs en beauté à ceux, qu'on voit en Sicile et dans la
, et qu'enfin cette grande, et majestueuse Architecture donne en son genre l'idée la plus parfaite de ce bel art.

Vue de ce qui reste encore des Murs A. de l'anciennne Ville de Pesto...
445 x 670 mm

Remains of the ancient city walls A. of Paestum
Überreste der antiken Stadtmauern A von Paestum
Vestiges des murs A. de l'ancienne ville de Paestum

Vue des restes du Pronaos de l'édifice, que l'on peut considérer comme le Collège des Anfictions
490 x 670 mm

View of the pronaos of the building known as the College of the Amphictyons
Ansicht vom Pronaos des als Kolleg der Amphiktyonia bekannten Gebäudes
Vue du pronaos de l'édifice dit Collège des Anfictions

Planche XI.

Temple de Neptune à Pesto, vu de côté, et dessiné plus en grand qu'on ne le voit dans la première planche.
Cav. Piranesi F.

Temple de Neptune à Pesto, vu de côté, et dessiné plus en grand qu'on ne le voit dans la première planche
455 x 673 mm

Side view of the temple of Neptune at Paestum

Seitenansicht des Neptun-Tempels in Paestum

Vue latérale du temple de Neptune à Paestum

Vue du temple de Neptune, Dieu tutélaire de l'ancienne Ville de Pesto,
480 x 707 mm

View of the temple of Neptune, tutelary god of Paestum
Tempel des Neptun, des Schutzgottes von Paestum
Vue du temple de Neptune, dieu protecteur de Paestum

Vue des restes interieurs d'un des Pronaos du Temple de Neptune qui regarde du côté de la Terre
495 x 670 mm

Interior view of one of the pronai facing inland
Innenansicht des landeinwärts ausgerichteten Pronaos
Vue d'un des pronaos orienté du côté de la terre

Vue d'un autre temple,
dans la Ville de Pesto,
que l'on croit commu-
nement avoir été dédié
à Junon
452 x 670 mm

View of another temple
of Paestum, probably
dedicated to Juno

Ansicht eines weiteren
Tempels in Paestum,
der vermutlich der Juno
geweiht war

Vue d'un autre temple
de Paestum, supposé
dédié à Junon

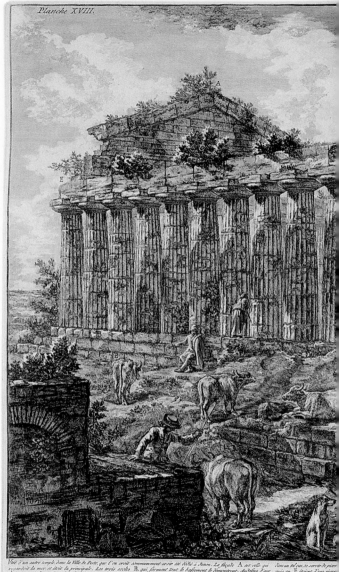

ru que le travertin, repondant de couches de pierre qui composent la paroi exterieure mar-
[...]ue lef. Cette pierre qui aujourd'hui tombe en pequisiere, fait bien voir qu'elle a etait qui
Celle s'etait fait à la carole pour mettre et de rarole sans les moyeux mais cela n'in
l'on n'approuvera, jamais que l'on substitua une pierre moins chere à une autre plus
devroit estre conduite le Stuc. Ce membre d'architecture detruit ici, semble conti-

rier l'ordre Dorique, et paroit plustost precaire de l'embaras, que de la legerete L'on aimeroit mieux un Laton, quelque
d'un siecle ancien, qu'une telle nouveaute. La corniche F est tellement ruinee, que l'on n'en peut prendre aucune idee
Celle De l'avant, en Fronton G en Scitures en partie, celle à Des saillies aussi à Des Lanterns. Ouvrages dont il n'est pas for
cible De rendre raison; le caprice sent avant Dessus l'archologie Dans son ancienne, Il est vraisemblable, que ce n'est pas
le meme, qui a construit le temple De Neptune, que l'on a decrit çy devant

Cav. Piranesi F.

Vedute di Roma disegnate ed incise da Giambattista Piranesi architetto veneziano

Title engraved on the title page: *Views of Rome drawn and etched by Giambattista Piranesi, Venetian Architect.*

The plates, executed over the course of Piranesi's career, from the second half of the 1740s until his death, were printed and sold as individual sheets or in collections that gradually increased as his output progressed, and occasionally included other series of prints as well.

Posthumous edition, bearing the same title, consisting of 135 prints engraved in 1778 plus 2 title pages. The additions consisted of the *Pianta di Roma e del Campo Marzio* and 2 plates by Francesco.

Editions Paris: Equivalent to the preceding ones plus 2 new plates by Francesco. All the plates are numbered 682–821. The copperplates are preserved at the Calcografia in Rome (vol. XVI–XVII).

In Francesco's *Catalogo* of his father's works, published in 1792, the year 1748 is indicated as the starting date for production of the Vedute, but research has confirmed that they were actually executed and published several years before. Among the various collections of the *Vedute* often combined together with other series during Piranesi's

Titel in das Titelblatt gestochen: *Ansichten von Rom gezeichnet und gestochen von Giambattista Piranesi, venezianischer Architekt.*

Die Platten, die seit der Mitte der vierziger Jahre bis zu Piranesis Tod entstanden, sind als Einzelblätter oder in Folgen gedruckt und verkauft worden. Einem Sammelwerk entsprechend nahm der Umfang zu, gelegentlich wurden auch Blätter anderer Ausgaben miteinbezogen.

Posthume Ausgabe unter dem gleichen Titel, die 135 bis zum Jahre 1778 gestochene Ansichten sowie zwei Titelblätter umfaßt. Diesen wurden die *Pianta di Roma e del Campo Marzio* sowie zwei Tafeln von Francesco hinzugefügt.

Ausgaben Paris: Sie stimmen mit der vorangegangenen überein und enthalten darüber hinaus zwei neue Tafeln von Francesco Piranesi. Die Platten sind von 682 bis 821 numeriert. Die Druckplatten werden in der Calcografia in Rom aufbewahrt (Bände XVI und XVII).

In der von Francesco Piranesi festgelegten Reihenfolge des Werkes seines Vaters, die der 1792 herausgegebene *Catalogo* überliefert, wird 1748 als das Jahr angegeben, in dem die Produktion der *Vedute* ihren Anfang nahm. Inzwischen kann es

Titre gravé sur le frontispice : *Vues de Rome dessinées et gravées par Giambattista Piranesi, architecte vénitien.*

Les plaques réalisées pendant toute la période d'activité de Piranesi, de la seconde moitié des années 1740 jusqu'à sa mort étaient imprimées et vendues séparément ou en recueils toujours plus importants au fil des années qui comprenaient parfois d'autres cycles d'estampes. Edition posthume avec le même titre et comprenant les 135 estampes gravées portant la date de 1778 plus les deux frontispices. Ont été ajoutées la *Pianta di Roma e del Campo Marzio* et deux planches gravées par Francesco.

Editions de Paris : Elles sont semblables à la précédente hormis deux nouvelles planches gravées par Francesco. Toutes les planches sont numérotées de 682 à 821. Les cuivres sont conservés à la Chalcographie de Rome (tomes XVI–XVII). Dans le classement de l'œuvre paternelle établi par Francesco et documenté par le Catalogue édité en 1792, l'année 1748 marque le début de la production des *Vedute*, mais les études piranésiennes ont permis de montrer que leur exécution effective et le début de leur diffusion sont antérieurs de quelques années.

life, particularly in the years between his definitive move to Rome and the publication of *Antichità Romane*, mention must be made of at least the 34 *Vedute* collected in 1751 by Bouchard in *Le Magnificenze di Roma le più remarcabili*, an edition that is so rare as to suggest that only a few copies were issued. The date of execution for each subject is indicated by their gradual appearance in the subsequent editions of the engraved *Catalogo delle Opere*, of which approximately 25 states are known from 1761 on. A printed list, inserted in the *Antichità Romane*, and thus datable to 1756, indicates that 39 were ready for sale at that time.

The *View of the remains of the fountainhead of the Acqua Giulia* had already appeared in the *Trofei di Ottaviano Augusto*, published in 1753.

als gesichert gelten, daß mit dem Druck und der Verbreitung bereits einige Jahre früher begonnen wurde. Aus der Vielzahl der oft mit anderen Folgen kombinierten *Vedute di Roma*, die zu Lebzeiten Piranesis und insbesondere in den Jahren zwischen seiner endgültigen Niederlassung in Rom und der Herausgabe der *Antichità Romane* erschienen, muß zumindest an die 34 *Vedute* erinnert werden, die Bouchard 1751 in *Le Magnificenze di Roma le più remarcabili* zusammengestellt hat. Die Ausgabe ist so selten, daß vermutlich nur sehr wenige Exemplare von ihr gedruckt wurden. Als Hinweis auf das Ausführungsdatum der einzelnen Motive mag die Auflistung in dem stets auf den aktuellen Stand gebrachten *Catalogo* gelten, von dem etwa 25 Zustände seit 1761 bekannt sind. Hingegen führt eine vom Herausgeber in die *Antichità Romane* aufgenommene, somit 1756 datierbare Liste bereits 39 käuflich zu erwerbende *Vedute* auf.

Die *Ansicht der Überreste des Kastells der Acqua Giulia* war zuvor schon in den 1753 erschienenen *Trofei di Ottaviano Augusto* veröffentlicht worden.

Parmi les multiples recueils de *Vedute* souvent mélangés avec d'autres séries durant la vie de Piranesi, et plus particulièrement pendant les années entre son installation définitive à Rome et la publication des *Antichità Romane*, il convient de s'arrêter sur les 34 *Vedute* réunies en 1751 par Bouchard dans *Le Magnificenze di Roma le più remarcabili*, édition si rare qu'on peut supposer qu'elle fut tirée à très peu d'exemplaires. L'unique élément de datation des planches séparées vient de leur apparition progressive dans les diverses mises à jour du *Catalogo* gravé dont on connaît 25 états à partir de 1761. Mais une liste typographiée, insérée dans les *Antichità Romane*, et datant de 1756, répertoriait déjà 39 *Vedute* disponibles à la vente.

La *Vue des vestiges de la fontaine de l'Acqua Giulia* avait déjà été imprimée dans les *Trofei di Ottaviano Augusto* parus en 1753.

Veduta del Monumento eretto dall'Imperador Tito Vespasiano per
aver ristaurati gl'Aquedotti dell'Acque dell'Aniene nuovo e
Claudia, essendovi scolpito in esso il nome di Claudio, che lo edi-
fico, e di Vespasiano, che lo restauro. 1. Aquedotto di Sisto V. che
conduce l'Acqua felice. 2. Forami fatti per introdurvi l'Aquedotto so-
pradetto. 3. Porte di Aureliano, o siano di Arcadio, ed Onorio fab-
bricate sovra varie macerie che in quel tempo coprivano l'an-

**Vedute di Roma
disegnate ed incise da
Giambattista Piranesi
Architetto Ve(nez)iano
400 x 540 mm**

Title page: Views of
Rome drawn and
etched by G. Piranesi,
Venetian Architect

Titelblatt: Ansichten
von Rom, gezeichnet
und gestochen von
G. Piranesi, venezia-
nischer Architekt

Page de titre : Vues de
Rome dessinées et
gravées par G. Piranesi,
architecte vénitien

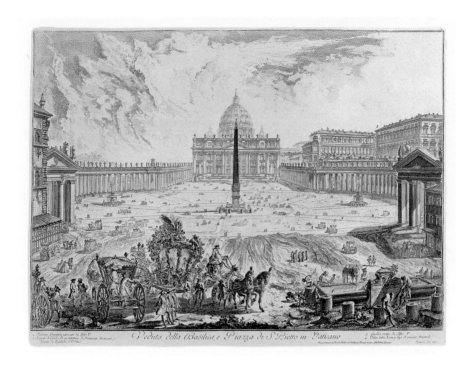

Veduta della Basilica, e Piazza di S. Pietro in Vaticano
380 x 540 mm

St. Peter's and the piazza of St. Peter's
St. Peter und der Petersplatz
La basilique St-Pierre et la place St-Pierre

Veduta interna della Basilica di S. Pietro in Vaticano

Veduta interna della Basilica di S. Pietro in Vaticano
385 x 595 mm

Interior view of St. Peter's
Innenansicht von St. Peter
Vue intérieure de St-Pierre

Veduta della Basilica di S.ᵗᵃ Maria Maggiore con le due Fabbriche laterali di detta Basilica

Veduta della Basilica di S.ᵗᵃ Maria Maggiore con le due Fabbriche laterali di detta Basilica
375 × 535 mm

View of S. Maria Maggiore
Ansicht von S. Maria Maggiore
Vue de Ste-Marie-Majeure

Veduta della Piazza del Popolo

Veduta della Piazza del Popolo
380 x 540 mm

View of the Piazza del Popolo
Ansicht der Piazza del Popolo
Vue de la piazza del Popolo

Veduta di Piazza Navona sopra le rovine del Circo Agonale
385 x 545 mm

View of Piazza Navona
Ansicht der Piazza Navona
Vue de la piazza Navona

1. Fontana fabbricata da Marc. Agrippa. 2. Fontana con quella Fontana architettura di Filippo Barigioni. 3. Dogana.

Veduta della Piazza della Rotonda

5. Pescaria
6. Palazzo Cresianzi

Piranesi N.

Veduta della Piazza della Rotonda
390 x 545 mm

View of the Piazza della Rotonda
Ansicht der Piazza della Rotonda
Vue de la piazza della Rotonda

Veduta della vasta Fontana di Trevi antica

Presso l'Autore a Strada Felice nel Palazzo Tomati vicino alla Trinità de' monti

Architettura di Nicola Sa

nte detta l'Acqua Vergine.

Piranesi del. Scul.

**Veduta della vasta
Fontana di Trevi
anticamente detta
l'Acqua Vergine
380 x 550 mm**

Trevi Fountain formerly
called the Acqua
Vergine

Fontana di Trevi, früher
Acqua Vergine genannt

Fontaine de Trevi
autrefois Acqua Vergine

Colonna Trajana
530 x 400

Trajan's column
Trajanssäule
La colonne de Trajan

Colonna Antonina
538 x 402 mm

The column of Marcus Aurelius
Die Mark Aurel-Säule
La colonne de Marc Aurèle

VEDUTA DELL' ESTERNO DELLA GRAN BASILICA DI S. PIETRO IN VATICANO

Veduta dell'esterno della gran Basilica di S. Pietro in Vaticano
380 x 600 mm

View of the exterior of St. Peter's
Außenansicht von St. Peter
Vue de l'extérieur de St-Pierre

Veduta di Piazza di Spagna
380 x 592 mm

View of the Piazza di Spagna
Ansicht der Piazza di Spagna
Vue de la piazza di Spagna

Veduta del Ponte e Castello Sant'Angelo

Veduta del Ponte e Castello Sant'Angelo
355 x 585 mm

View of the Castel S. Angelo and bridge
Ansicht der Engelsbrücke und der Engelsburg
Vue du pont et du château Saint-Ange

VEDUTA DEGLI AVANZI DEL TABLINO DELLA CASA AUREA DI NERONE, DETTI VOLGARMENTE IL TEMPIO DELLA PACE

1 Di qui fu trasportata da Paolo V. la gran Colonna che si vede innalzata nella Piazza di S. Maria Maggiore.   2 Muri, e piloni che reggevano la parte opposta del Tablino.   3 Nicchie per le Statue degli uomini illustri.

Veduta degli avanzi del Tablino della Casa Aurea di Nerone, detti volgarmente il Tempio della Pace
400 x 550 mm

View of remains of the dining room of the Golden House of Nero
Ansicht der Überreste des Speisesaals der Domus Aurea des Nero, gewöhnlich Tempio della Pace genannt
Vue des vestiges de la salle à manger de la Domus Aurea dit Tempio della Pace

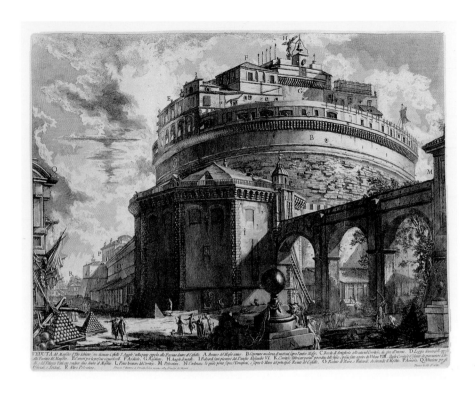

VEDUTA del Mausoleo d'Elio Adriano (ora chiamato Castello S. Angelo) nella parte opposta alla Piazza Amore al Castello. A Avanzo del Masio antico. B Coperture moderna di mattoni sopra l'antico Masio. C Inzola di Anfiteatro nell'estrado dell'ortile, de qua all'interno. D Loggia dinanzi alle... [illegible Italian legend text]

Veduta del Mausoleo d'Elio Adriano (ora chiamato Castello S. Angelo) nella parte opposta ...
415 x 555 mm

Rear view of the mausoleum of Hadrian (Castel S. Angelo)
Rückansicht des Hadrian-Mausoleums (Engelsburg)
Le mausolée d'Hadrien vu de dos (château Saint-Ange)

Veduta della Facciata di dietro della Basilica di S. Maria Maggiore

Veduta della Facciata di dietro della Basilica di S. Maria Maggiore
375 x 610 mm

Rear view of the basilica of S. Maria Maggiore
Rückansicht der Basilika S. Maria Maggiore
La basilique Ste-Marie-Majeure vue de dos

A *Archi del prim' Ordine dell' Anfiteatro, pe' quali il popolo ascendeva ai gradi dopo Spettacoli.*
B *Recinto moderno.* C *Numeri incisi negli esterni archi, sono e più segno di chi desiderava d'esser rinnovata fra la moltitudine degli Spettatori.* D *Arco senza numero, sopra cui era immaginato il ponte che dalle fabbriche Cesaree dell' Esquilino dava l'ingresso nell' Anfit.* E *Parte dell' Anfit. deturpata dagl'Incendy.*

Veduta dell' Anfiteatro Flavio,

Presso l'Autore a Strada Felice vicino alla Trinità de Monti.

il Colofseo

V. Archi del secondo e terz' ordine anticamente internachiuse dà parapetti, de' quali si restano alcuni segni e
rovine. G. Mensole sin cui posavano le antenne di metallo, che, passando per la cornice, sostenevano la gran
tenda. H. Arola ove interrotte dalle antenne, nelle quali ora impressa la parte interrotta del medesima.
I. Radici del monte Esquilino. K. Arco di Costantino. L. Monte Celio. M. Principio della via di S. Gio. Laterano.

**Veduta dell'Anfiteatro
Flavio, detto il Colosseo**
405 x 685 mm

View of the Flavian
Amphitheater, called
the Colosseum

Ansicht des Flavischen
Amphitheaters,
genannt Kolosseum

Vue de l'amphithéâtre
Flavien, dit le Colisée

Altra veduta del tempio della Sibilla in Tivoli
620 x 435 mm

Another view of the Sibylline Temple at Tivoli
Andere Ansicht des Sibyllen-Tempels in Tivoli
Autre vue du temple de la Sibylle à Tivoli

Veduta interna del Tempio della Tosse…
550 x 625 mm

Interior view of the Tempio della Tosse
Innenansicht des Tempio della Tosse
Vue intérieure du temple della Tosse

**Veduta interna della
Villa di Mecenate
470 x 675 mm**

Interior view of the villa
of Maecenas

Innenansicht der
Maecenas-Villa

Vue intérieure de la
villa de Mécène

Veduta dell'Arco di Costantino
470 x 705 mm

View of the arch of Constantine
Ansicht des Konstantinsbogens
Vue de l'arc de Constantin

Veduta dell'Arco di Settimio Severo
465 x 700 mm

View of the arch of Septimius Severus
Ansicht des Septimius-Severus-Bogens
Vue de l'arc de Septime Sévère

**Veduta della Villa Estnse
in Tivoli**
460 x 690 mm

View of the Villa d'Este
in Tivoli

Ansicht der Villa d'Este
in Tivoli

Vue de la villa d'Este à
Tivoli

Biography · Biographie · Biographie

4.10.1720
Giambattista Piranesi is born in
Venice to Angelo and Laura
Lucchesi. He is christened on
8 November in the church of
S. Moisè.

Giambattista Piranesi wird in Venedig als Sohn von Angelo und Laura
Lucchesi geboren. Am 8. November
wird er in der Kirche S. Moisè
getauft.

Fils d'Angelo et de Laura Lucchesi,
Giambattista Piranesi, dit Piranèse
naît à Venise. Il est baptisé le 8
novembre en l'église S. Moisè.

c. 1735–1740
Trains first as an architect under
Matteo Lucchesi and Giovanni
Antonio Scalfarotto, then studies
etching with Carlo Zucchi in
Venice.

Ausbildung zunächst bei den
Architekten Matteo Lucchesi und
Giovanni Antonio Scalfarotto,
später bei dem Kupferstecher Carlo
Zucchi in Venedig.

Formation d'architecte chez Matteo
Lucchesi et Govanni Antonio
Scalfarotto, puis chez le graveur
Carlo Zucchi à Venise.

1740
Travels to Rome in the
entourage of the new Venetian
ambassador Francesco Venier and
probably lives in the Palazzo
Venezia.

In der Gefolgschaft des neuen
venezianischen Botschafters
Francesco Venier reist Piranesi
nach Rom und wohnt wahr-
scheinlich im Palazzo Venezia.

Faisant partie de la suite du nouvel
ambassadeur vénitien Francesco
Venier, Piranesi part pour Rome et
réside probablement au palazzo
Venezia.

1740–1742
Short training as a stage
designer under Domenico and
Giuseppe Valeriani. Makes
regular visits to the studio of the
Sicilian artist Giuseppe Vasi and
begins the first plates of his
*Prima Parte di Architetture, e
Prospettive*.

Kurze Ausbildung zum
Bühnenbildner bei Domenico und
Giuseppe Valeriani. Besucht
regelmäßig das Atelier des
Sizilianers Giuseppe Vasi und
beginnt mit den ersten Tafeln der
*Prima Parte di Architetture, e
Prospettive*.

Bref apprentissage chez Domenico
et Giuseppe Valeriani, peintres de
décors de théâtre. Fréquente
régulièrement l'atelier du Sicilien
Giuseppe Vasi et commence les
premières planches de *Prima Parte
di Architetture, e Prospettive*.

1743
The first part of the *Prima Parte
di Architetture, e Prospettive*
appears in July with a dedication
to Nicola Giobbe. Probably
makes his first short trip to
Naples.

Im Juli diesen Jahres erscheint
die erste Folge der *Prima Parte di
Architetture, e Prospettive* mit der
Widmung an Nicola Giobbe.
Wahrscheinlich erste kurze
Neapelreise.

Dédicacée à Nicola Giobbe, la
première série de *Prima Parte di
Architetture, e Prospettive* paraît au
mois de juillet de cette année.
Entreprend probablement son
premier bref voyage à Naples.

1744
Publishes *The royal villa
Ambrosiana*, which is republished
in the series *Vedute delle Ville e
d'altri luoghi della Toscana* by
Giuseppe Allegrini in Florence.

Er publiziert *Die königliche Villa
Ambrosiana*, die in der Folge *Vedute
delle Ville e d'altri luoghi della
Toscana* in Florenz von Giuseppe
Allegrini herausgegeben wird. Von

Publie *La villa royale de
l'Ambrosiana* qui est éditée à
Florence par Giuseppe Allegrini à la
suite de *Vedute delle Ville e d'altri
luoghi della Toscana*.

Stays in Venice from May
to September.

Mai bis September hält er sich in
Venedig auf.

Réside à Venise de mai à
septembre.

October 1744–May 1745
Works with Carlo Nolli in Rome on
the *Pianta del corso del Tevere*. His
*Varie vedute di Roma Antica e
Moderna* appear in 1745 and are
later reprinted in further editions.

Zurück in Rom arbeitet er mit
Carlo Nolli am Pianta del corso del
Tevere. Im Jahre 1745 erscheinen
die *Varie vedute di Roma Antica e
Moderna*, von denen im Verlauf der
nächsten Jahre weitere Ausgaben
erscheinen.

Travaille à Rome à la *Pianta del
corso del Tevere* avec Carlo Nolli. En
1745 paraissent les *Varie vedute di
Roma Antica e Moderna* dont seront
tirées plusieurs éditions au cours
des années suivantes.

July 1745–August 1747
Piranesi lives in Venice and begins
the first series of *Carceri*.

Piranesi lebt in Venedig und
beginnt mit der ersten Serie der
Carceri.

Piranesi vit à Venise et commence
la première série des *Carceri*.

1747
Returns to Rome in September and
moves into the Via del Corso,
opposite Palazzo Mancini, seat of
the French Academy. In the
autumn he embarks on the massive
work *Vedute di Roma*, which
occupies him for the rest of his life,
and also begins the *Antichità
romane de'tempi della Repubblica*.

Im September diesen Jahres ist er
wieder in Rom und wohnt an der
Via del Corso gegenüber vom
Palazzo Mancini, Sitz der französi-
schen Akademie. Im Herbst beginnt
er mit den großen *Vedute di Roma*,
an denen er bis an sein Lebensende
arbeiten wird, sowie mit den *Antichità romane de'tempi della Repubblica*.

Est de nouveau à Rome en
septembre et habite dans la via del
Corso en face du palazzo Mancini,
siège de l'Académie de France. A
l'automne, entrepend les grandes
Vedute di Roma, sur lesquelles il
travaillera jusqu'à la fin de sa vie,
ainsi que les *Antichità romane
de'tempi della Repubblica*.

1748
Collaborates with Giovanni Battista
Nolli on the *Nuova pianta di Roma*
and publishes the series *Antichità
romane de'tempi della Repubblica, e
de'primi imperatori*.

Er arbeitet mit Giovanni Battista
Nolli am *Nuova pianta di Roma* und
gibt die Folge der *Antichità romane
de'tempi della Repubblica, e de'primi
imperatori* heraus.

Travaille avec Giovanni Battista
Nolli à la *Nuova pianta di Roma* et
publie la série des *Antichità romane
de'tempi della Repubblica, e de'primi
imperatori*.

1750
The series of plates *Opere Varie di
Architettura, prospettive, grotteschi*,
some of which have already been
printed, is published by Giovanni
Bouchard.

Im Verlag von Giovanni Bouchard
erscheint die Folge *Opere Varie di
Architettura, prospettive, grotteschi*.
Einige Tafeln sind bereits vorher
erschienen.

Publication de la série *Opere Varie
di Architettura, prospettive, grotteschi*
chez l'éditeur Giovanni Bouchard.
Certaines planches ont déjà été
éditées au préalable.

1751
Publication of *Le Magnificenze di
Roma*.

Publikation der Veduten-Folge *Le
Magnificenze di Roma*.

Publication de la série
Le Magnificenze di Roma.

1752

Piranesi marries Angela Pasquini and publishes the *Raccolta di varie vedute di Roma*.

Piranesi heiratet Angela Pasquini und publiziert die *Raccolta di varie vedute di Roma*.

Piranesie épouse Angela Pasquini et publie la *Raccolta di varie vedute di Roma*.

1753

Publication of the *Trofei di Ottaviano Augusto*.

Es erscheinen die *Trofei di Ottaviano Augusto*.

Publication des *Trofei di Ottaviano Augusto*.

1756

The first part of the four-volume edition of *Antichità Romane* is published.

Der erste Band der vierbändigen Ausgabe der *Antichità Romane* erscheint.

Publication du premier des quatre volumes des *Antichità Romane*.

1757

Made an honorary member of the Society of Antiquarians in London. Publication of the *Lettere di Giustificazione*.

Er wird Ehrenmitglied der Society of Antiquarians in London. Es erscheinen die *Lettere di Giustificazione*.

Est fait membre honoraire de la Société des antiquaires de Londres. Publication des *Lettere di Giustificazione*.

1758/59

Birth of Piranesi's son, Francesco.

Der Sohn Francesco wird geboren.

Naissance de son fils Francesco.

1761

Moves into the Palazzo Tomati in the Strada Felice, now known as the Via Sistina, and publishes perhaps his best-known series of plates, the *Carceri*, as well as the edition *Della Magnificenza ed Architettura de'Romani*. Elected to the Accademico di San Luca that same year.

Er bezieht den Palazzo Tomati an der Strada Felice, der heutigen Via Sistina, und publiziert seine vielleicht bekannteste Folge, die *Carceri*, sowie *Della Magnificenza ed Architettura de'Romani*. Im gleichen Jahr wird er zum Accademico di San Luca ernannt.

S'installe au palazzo Tomati dans la strada Felice, aujourd'hui via Sistina, et publie les *Carceri*, sans doute sa série la plus célèbre, ainsi que *Della Magnificenza ed Architettura de'Romani*. Il est nommé la même année académicien de Saint-Luc.

1762

Publication of the *Lapides Capitolini*, *Il Campo Marzio* and the *Descrizione e Disegno dell'Emissario del Lago Albano*.

Es erscheinen die *Lapides Capitolini*, *Il Campo Marzio* sowie die *Descrizione e Disegno dell'Emissario del Lago Albano*.

Publication de *Lapides Capitolini*, *Il Campo Marzio* ainsi que de *Descrizione e Disegno dell'Emissario del Lago Albano*.

1764

Publishes the *Antichità d'Albano e di Castel Gandolfo, Blackfriars Bridge in London, The Works in Architecture* and the *Raccolta di alcuni disegni del Guercino*. Around this time, the *Antichità di Cora* also appear. Wins a contract to restore the church S. Maria del Priorato on the Aventin.

Er publiziert die *Antichità d'Albano e di Castel Gandolfo, Blackfriars Bridge in London, The Works in Architecture* und die *Raccolta di alcuni disegni del Guercino*. Etwa im gleichen Zeitraum erscheinen auch die *Antichità di Cora*. Er erhält den Auftrag, die Kirche S. Maria del Priorato auf dem Aventin zu restaurieren.

Publie *Antichità d'Albano e di Castel Gandolfo, Blackfriars Bridge in London, The Works in Architecture* et *Raccolta di alcuni disegni del Guercino*. Les *Antichità di Cora* paraissent à peu près à la même époque. Est chargé de restaurer l'église S. Maria del Priorato sur l'Aventin.

1765

Publication of the *Osservazioni sopra la lettre de M. Mariette*. The series of

Es erscheinen die *Osservazioni sopra la lettre de M. Mariette*. Die Folge *Le*

Publication des *Osservazioni sopra la lettre de M. Mariette*. La série *Le*

plates *Le Antichità romane de'Tempi della Repubblica* are republished with new numbering under the title *Alcune vedute di Archi Trionfali.*

Antichità romane de'tempi della Repubblica wird ein weiteres Mal mit neuer Numerierung unter dem Titel *Alcune vedute di Archi Trionfali* publiziert.

Antichità romane de'tempi della Repubblica est rééditée avec une nouvelle numérotation sous le titre *Alcune vedute di Archi Trionfali.*

1766
Piranesi completes the restoration of S. Maria del Priorato.

Piranesi beendet die Restaurierungsarbeiten in S. Maria del Priorato.

Piranesi achève les travaux de restauration de S. Maria del Priorato.

1767
Works on the Quirinal Palace for Cardinal Rezzonico and makes drawings of the ruins of Hadrian's Villa in Tivoli.

Er arbeitet im Quirinalspalast für Kardinal Rezzonico und zeichnet die Ruinen der Hadriansvilla in Tivoli.

Travaille au Quirinal pour le cardinal Rezzonico et dessine les ruines de la villa Adriana à Tivoli.

1769
Publication of the *Diverse Maniere d'adornare i cammini.*

Es erscheinen die *Diverse Maniere d'adornare i cammini.*

Publication des *Diverse Maniere d'adornare i cammini.*

1770
First of many visits to Pompeii and Herculaneum.

Erster von zahlreichen Besuchen in Pompeji und Herculaneum.

Première visite suivie de beaucoup d'autres de Pompei et Herculanum.

1773–1775
Illustrations of the *Trajan's Column* and *Antoninus' Column* are published under the title *Trofeo o sia Magnifica Colonna Coclide di marmo.*

Es erscheinen die Darstellungen der Trajanssäule und der Antoninussäule unter dem Titel Trofeo o sia Magnifica Colonna Coclide di marmo.

Les représentations de la *Colonne de Trajan* et de la *Colonne d'Antonin* sont publiées sous le titre *Trofeo o sia Magnifica Colonna Coclide di marmo.*

1777
Travels to Pesto, where he makes drawings of the temple precincts.

Er reist nach Paestum und zeichnet die Tempelanlagen.

Voyage à Paestum pour y dessiner les temples.

1778
Publication of the *Pianta di Roma e del Camp Marzio* and *Vasi, candelabri, cippi, sarcophagi.* Piranesi begins the *Différentes vues de Pesto* but dies on 9 November in Rome.

Es erscheinen der Pianta di Roma e del Campo Marzio sowie die Vasi, candelabri, cippi, sarcophagi, und er beginnt mit den Différentes vues de Pesto. Am 9. November stirbt Piranesi in Rom.

Publication de *Pianta di Roma e del Campo Marzio,* et les *Vasi, candelabri, cippi, sarcophagi.* Commence les *Différentes vues de Pesto.* Piranesi meurt le 9 novembre à Rome.

1784
The printers Salomoni, on the Piazza S. Ignazio, publish the 2nd edition of the *Antichità Romane.*

Die Druckerei Salomoni an der Piazza S. Ignazio publiziert die 2. Ausgabe der Antichità Romane.

L'imprimerie Salomoni sur la piazza S. Ignazio publie la deuxième édition des *Antichità Romane.*

1792
Publication of a complete catalogue of Piranesi's works.

Es erscheint der Gesamtkatalog seiner Werke.

Publication du catalogue rassemblant toutes ses œuvres.

Index

COVER/BACK COVER:
Studies of Etruscan friezes at Chiusi (detail)

© 2001   TASCHEN GmbH
Hohenzollernring 53, D–50672 Köln
www.taschen.com

© 2001   Ministero per i Beni e le Attività Culturali/
Istituto Nazionale per la Grafica, Roma

© 2001   for all photographs:
Archivio Fotografico dell'Istituto Nazionale per la Grafica, Roma

EDITING   Thierry Nebois, Cologne
DESIGN   Claudia Frey, Cologne
COVER DESIGN   Angelika Taschen, Cologne
PRODUCTION   Horst Neuzner, Cologne
ENGLISH TRANSLATION   Bradley Baker Dick, Rome
GERMAN TRANSLATION   Verena Listl, Rome
FRENCH TRANSLATION   Isabelle Baraton, Paris

Printed in Italy
ISBN 3–8228–5530–8

"Buy them all and add some pleasure to your life."

www.taschen.com